Christian Issues in the Gospels

Also published by Stanley Thornes

Eileen Bromley   *The Gospels: A GCSE Activities Pack*
The Gospels Today: An Approach to the Synoptic Gospels for GCSE
Judaism: A GCSE Activities Pack

CHRISTIAN ISSUES IN THE GOSPELS

Eileen Bromley

Formerly Head of RE, Southfield School for Girls, Kettering

To Paul

Very best wishes

Eileen

Stanley Thornes (Publishers) Ltd

First published in 1991 by:
Stanley Thornes (Publishers) Ltd
Old Station Drive
Leckhampton
CHELTENHAM GL53 0DN
England

British Library Cataloguing in Publication Data

Bromley, Eileen
 Christian issues in the gospels.
 I. Title
 230

ISBN 07487-0582 1

Typeset by Tech-Set, Gateshead, Tyne & Wear.
Printed and bound in Great Britain by Ebenezer Baylis & Son Ltd, Worcester.

Contents

Introduction

This book is an introduction to the origins, in the Synoptic Gospels, of contemporary Christian beliefs, practices and attitudes. The material may be used as part of an examination course or as a basis for a general Religious Studies course in the upper secondary school.

Christian Issues in the Gospels attempts to fulfil the requirement that, at GCSE level, religious texts should be seen as 'authoritative documents which are used to guide and inspire the faithful today' (*Religious Studies GCSE: A Guide for Teachers,* SEC, 1986). It is therefore relevant to the GCSE syllabuses on the Gospels and, used in conjunction with *The Gospels Today: An Approach to the Synoptic Gospels for GCSE,* gives a comprehensive coverage of all the syllabuses on the Gospels. The material is also appropriate for syllabuses on Christianity, and Section D is particularly relevant to the Christian Perspectives/Contemporary Issues syllabuses of the various GCSE boards.

It is important that the Gospel references should be studied at the beginning of each Topic. *The Gospels Today* will give help in the understanding of the text. The introduction to each Topic is deliberately brief, and includes source material from a wide variety of Christian traditions. The emphasis is on student research and discussion. Some of the suggested activities are suitable as starting points for coursework. Any links which can be made with local churches and individual Christians will prove invaluable in helping students to consider the Gospel texts as 'a living element in the Christian community today' (Ibid.).

Acknowledgements

The author wishes to thank the following for their help in the preparation of the manuscript:

Margaret Bacon, Revd Norman Barr, Rose Barr, Reg Cartwright, Barry Clark, Geoff Crowther, Canon Michael Farrer, Father Keith Frisby, Revd Rob Frost, Revd Barrie Hirst, John Masding, Revd Fred Pritchard, Sarah and David Wheeler, Canon Dick Williams and Kibworth Methodist Youth Fellowship.

The author and publishers would like to thank the following for permission to reproduce photographs and illustrations:

Revd Norman Barr, p. 18 (right) • Camera Press, p. 50 • Andrew Carpenter, p. 35 • Reg Cartwright, p. 3 • Cephas, p. 21 • Christian Aid, p. 56 • Church Missionary Society, p. 11 (bottom left) • Barry Clark, p. 29 • Coventry City Council, p. 9 • Geoff Crowther, p. 22 • Keith Ellis, pp. 19, 28, 37 • Canon Michael Farrer, p. 18 (left) • Format, p. 57 • Sally and Richard Greenhill, p. 47 • HEED Bangladesh, p. 56 (Logo) • Kingsway Publications/Image Bank, p. 23 • Knights of St. Columba, p. 36 • Leprosy Mission/Donald A Michael, p. 11 (top) • Hugh J McGough, p. 6 • Methodist Church Overseas Division, pp. 16 (Catherine Ibbotson), 25 (Mark Howard), 41 (John Pritchard), 51, 55 (left, Dr Andrew Pearson; right, Jan Pickard) • Methodist Publishing House, p. 5 • Methodist Recorder, p. 7 • National Children's Home, p. 46 • Trustees of the National Gallery, London, p. 31 • Oxfam, p. 56 (Logo) • Pacemaker, p. 49 • Palm Tree Press/ Arthur Baker. Used by permission from the Instant Art Series, Licence No. 099052, p. 32 • Popperfoto, pp. 11 (bottom right), 53 • RNLI, p. 13 • Salvation Army, p. 60 • Science Photo Library, p. 1 • Tear Fund, p. 56 (Logo and Poster), 59 • John Twinning, p. 33 • War on Want, p. 56

Also the following for permission to reproduce copyright material:

Baptist Times for the extract, page 52 • Bible Society/Collins for biblical quotations, all from the *Good News Bible* • Central Board of Finance of the Church of England for extracts from *The Alternative Service Book (1980)* • Collins for the extracts from *Miracles* and the Preface to *The Screwtape Letters* by C S Lewis, pages 3 and 40, and the extract from *Mother Teresa: Her People and Her Work* by Desmond Doig, page 50 • *Daily Telegraph* for the letter, page 21 • *Harborough Herald and Post* for the letter, page 30 • *Harborough Mail* for the article on page 35 • International Committee on English in the Liturgy, Inc. for excerpts from the English translation of *The Roman Missal* (c) 1973. All rights reserved • Logos Books for the prayer from *Prayers of Life*, page 53 • Methodist Publishing House for prayers and hymns from *The Methodist Service Book (1975)* • *Methodist Recorder* for the articles on pages 34 and 37 ('My Second Easter') • *Oadby and Wigston Mail* for the article on page 37 ('Holy Story to be re-enacted') • Revd Fred Pritchard for the account 'I was in prison and you visited me', page 50 • Thank You Music for verses from the hymn *The Servant King* by Graham Kendrick, page 61 • Josef Weinberger Ltd for the verses of the hymn *Lord Jesus Christ*, page 8 • Canon R H L Williams for the extract from *God Thoughts*, page 1, and the prayers from *Prayers for Today's Church*, pages 26, 42, 47, 52 and 54.

Cover photographs are reproduced by permission of Andes Press Agency/Carlos Reyes, and Ateliers et Presses de Taizé, France.

God

I believe in God, the Father almighty,
creator of heaven and earth . . .

The Apostles' Creed

Read *Mark* 12:24–7, 29–31
Luke 12:29–32, 20:37–8
Matthew 5:48, 6:8–9, 31–3, 7:21, 11:25–7, 22:31–2, 37–8

❛I am an atheist.❜

❛I believe in God.❜

❛I am a Christian.❜

❛I am a Jew.❜

❛I am a Muslim.❜

❛I am an agnostic.❜

❛I am a theist.❜

❛I believe in Jesus Christ.❜

> *. . . Is there a language, Lord, by which you can speak to us – your Great Person to us small ones? The Bible says that you have spoken to us in Jesus Christ. That you spoke in different ways at different times, but eventually you spoke with full authority in and through Jesus Christ. Can this be true?*
>
> Dick Williams, *God Thoughts*

Problems concerning belief in God were not as real for the first Christians as they are for many people today. Most of the followers of Jesus had a Jewish background and accepted the existence of an eternal, almighty God and creator.

A new emphasis in the teaching of Jesus was on the Fatherhood of God. He encouraged his followers to realise that they could have a relationship with the almighty God as children with a father, a relationship of trust and love. They were taught that prayer is communication with God the Father, who already understands his children's needs.

It was further claimed in Matthew's Gospel (11:27) that the Father could only be known through his Son, Jesus. Having met Jesus, and believing that he was the Son through whom they could know the Father, the first Christians did not see any need to argue for God's existence.

'Before you . . . brought the world into being, you were eternally God, and will be God forever.'
Psalm 90:2

ACTIVITIES

1 Find out the meaning of these words: theist, atheist, agnostic. Discuss the difference between a theist and a Christian.

2 Within your group, carry out an anonymous survey on belief in God. First write either:
    'I believe in God . . .' or
    'I do not believe in God . . .' or
    'I don't know whether I believe in God or not . . .'
Then give reasons for what you have written. Discuss the results of the survey.

3 Ask your family and friends whether they believe in God. Make brief notes of the replies and construct a class chart of the beliefs stated.

4 Gather together as much evidence as you can:
    a) for the existence of God
    b) against the existence of God.
    Discuss it.

5 Discuss why belief in God is more of a problem for some people today than it was for the first Christians.

6 Look up Luke 12:22–31 or Matthew 6:25–34 and then answer the following questions:
    a) What title is used of God in this passage?
    b) Give an example of another well-known passage where this title is used.
    c) What was Jesus' answer to the question 'Which commandment is the most important of all?'
    d) What does the above passage suggest about an answer to the problem of worry?
    e) How, according to the Gospels, could a person enter into a relationship with God? Do you think this is still possible today?

7 Discuss the quotation from Dick Williams' *God Thoughts*.

The Incarnation

*. . . He was conceived by the power of the Holy Spirit
and born of the Virgin Mary . . .*

The Apostles' Creed

Read *Luke* 1:26–38
 Matthew 1:18–25

The belief that Jesus was actually the Son of God and that Joseph played no part in his conception was accepted at an early point in the history of Christianity and became part of the Apostles' Creed and of other statements of belief. Some people today believe that Jesus was the son of Joseph and Mary, who lived a perfect life; the only human being ever to do so. For most Christians, however, the belief in the Incarnation (that God became man) is central to their faith.

The doctrine of the Incarnation suggests that the Son of God took human flesh when he was born of Mary, so that he was both God and Man.

Christians believe that Jesus was therefore sinless and able to mount a divine rescue operation in order to provide sinful human beings with 'salvation'. This belief is expressed in a well-known eighteenth century Christmas hymn, 'Hark! the herald-angels sing.'

> *The central miracle asserted by Christians is the Incarnation. They say that God became Man. Every other miracle prepares for this, or exhibits this, or results from this.*
>
> C.S. Lewis, *Miracles*

ACTIVITIES

1 The unusual Christmas card opposite is an interpretation of the Christmas message. Discuss its meaning.

2 Find a copy of 'Hark! the herald-angels sing' and make notes about its contents under the headings:
   a) Teaching from the Gospels
   b) Christian beliefs
   c) Exhortations (encouragements) to worship.

This exercise can be carried out on other Christmas hymns and carols.

3 Collect Christmas cards and select those which:
   a) show a Nativity scene
   b) interpret the story, as the card above does.

Display the cards, with your comments.

4 Discuss C.S. Lewis' statement about the Incarnation. What do you think he is suggesting about miracles?

5 Read again the passages from the Gospels and then answer the following questions:
   a) From whose point of view is the story told by (i) Luke, (ii) Matthew?
   b) What was unusual about the conception of the child?
   c) What is the significance of the names suggested for the child?
   d) What different interpretations do Christians put on these stories today?
   e) What do you understand by the words 'the Christian belief in the Incarnation'?

Who is Jesus?

*'I believe in Jesus Christ,
his only Son, our Lord.'*

The Apostles' Creed

Read *Mark* 1:1, 9–11, 4:35–41, 6:14–16, 8:27–9:13
Luke 1:26–35, 3:21–3, 7:18–34, 8:22–5, 9:7–9, 18–36
Matthew 1:18–23, 3:13–17, 8:23–7, 11:2–6, 16:13–28, 17:1–13

By the time the Gospels were written the early Christians had reached important conclusions about the identity of the man they had known as Jesus of Nazareth. Their faith is stated by Mark in the title of his Gospel (Mark 1:1). There was significance even in Jesus' name (Matthew 1:21), and the Gospels trace the gradual way in which the disciples came to have faith in him. On one occasion, after experiencing his power over nature, they asked each other 'Who is this man?' They eventually reached their conclusion, which was stated by Peter on behalf of all of them, 'You are the Messiah'. Matthew adds '. . . the Son of the living God'.

This belief that Jesus was the Messiah or Christ, and the Son of God, is evident in the Gospels. It was soon to become part of the creeds of the Church, including the Apostles' Creed. Throughout the centuries, Christians have stated this belief in various ways.

You may have seen a fish used on a badge, brooch or necklace and wondered what it symbolised.

During times of persecution, the early Christians developed this as a secret sign to proclaim that they were disciples of Jesus. A fish drawn with two quick strokes in the dust identified them as Christians. The Greek word for fish is ιχθυς (*ichthus*). The Greek letters are used to form an *acrostic* the words of which summarise what Christians believe about Jesus:

ι	*ie*sous	Jesus
χ	*ch*ristos	Christ
θ	*th*eou	God's
υ	*u*ios	Son
ς	*s*oter	Saviour

Christians today believe that the answer to the question 'Who is Jesus?' is central to their faith. The fish symbol is still used by many Christian groups as an expression of their faith in Jesus.

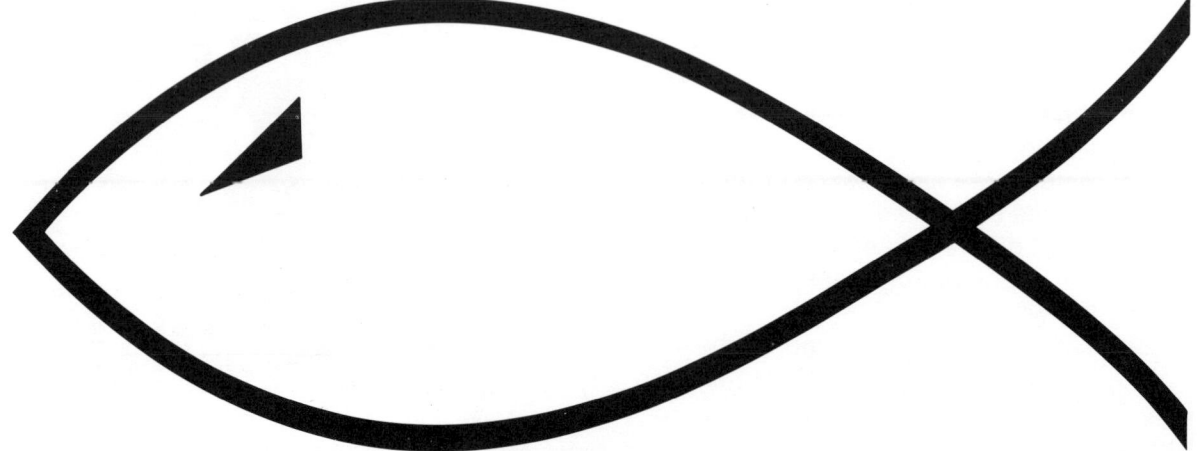

ACTIVITIES

1 Answer the following questions:
   a) Why is the fish such an appropriate symbol of Christian discipleship?
   b) How did the use of the fish symbol originate?
   c) Explain carefully the meaning which has become associated with the word *ichthus*.

2 Look out for examples of the use of a fish as a Christian symbol. Make a note of any that you find.

3 Look up again Mark 8:27–9, Luke 9:18–20 or Matthew 16:13–16 and answer the following questions:
   a) What conclusions had the disciples reached about Jesus?
   b) What conclusions had other people reached? (Use material from other passages mentioned in this Topic.)
   c) Suggest ways in which Christians might show their faith in Jesus today.

4 Ask a number of people, Christians and non-Christians, what they believe about who Jesus is. Present your results as a chart.

5 Find about six different Christian prayers or hymns. Discuss what they suggest about who Jesus is.

The Atonement

He suffered under Pontius Pilate, was crucified,
died and was buried.

The Apostles' Creed

Read *Mark* 14:22–6, 15:33–41
      Luke 22:14–20, 23:44–9
      Matthew 26:26–9, 27:45–56

❛I see you're wearing the symbol of a murder round your neck again – it's really gruesome!❜

❛It's only a piece of jewellery. It doesn't mean anything.❜

❛Perhaps not for you, but I saw a vicar wearing a cross the other day. And why do you see crosses on churches? It's morbid . . .❜

A cross is the most important symbol of Christianity. Christians believe that something very significant happened when Jesus died; that his death made it possible for sinful human beings to be reconciled to a holy God (made at one with him). This teaching is known as the doctrine of the Atonement.

At the Last Supper, Jesus talked of '. . . my blood which is poured out for many for the forgiveness of sins'. There are hints in the

5

Gospels that, rather than being seen as a tragic miscarriage of justice, the death of Jesus is to be seen as an expression of the love of God for humanity, breaking down barriers between God and people, and providing salvation and forgiveness of sins. Christians see important symbolism in the tearing of the Temple curtain, which separated the Holy of Holies from the rest of the Temple. A way had been made for human beings to approach God, and to enter into a closer relationship with him.

Here are the words of one of the best-known hymns about the Crucifixion, which express the doctrine of the Atonement in simple language:

There is a green hill far away
Without a city wall,
Where the dear Lord was crucified
Who died to save us all.

We may not know, we cannot tell
What pains he had to bear;
But we believe it was for us
He hung and suffered there.

He died that we might be forgiven,
He died to make us good,
That we might go at last to heaven,
Saved by His precious blood.

There was no other good enough
To pay the price of sin;
He only could unlock the gate
Of heaven, and let us in.

O dearly, dearly has he loved,
And we must love Him too,
And trust in His redeeming blood,
And try His works to do.

Cecil Frances Alexander

ACTIVITIES

1 What does the above hymn suggest about the purpose of Jesus' death?

2 Use hymn and service books to find other hymns or prayers that express the doctrine of the Atonement.

3 Answer the following questions:
   a) Where was Jesus crucified?
   b) What happened in the Temple at the time of Jesus' death?
   c) What significance do Christians see in what happened there?
   d) What aspect of the Crucifixion do you think is emphasised by the illustration opposite?
   e) Why do you think some people today wear crosses?
   f) What do you think is meant by 'the doctrine of the Atonement'?

4 Look for any crosses you can find in your community. If possible, sketch them and make a note of their type and purpose.

This detail of a banner, created for the Methodist Church, Sherborne by Margaret Bacon, is an interpretation of the Crucifixion

The Resurrection

. . . On the third day he rose again.

The Apostles' Creed

Read   *Mark* 16:1–20
        Luke 24:1–49
        Matthew 28:1–20

Soon after the death of Jesus, the first disciples became convinced that he had risen. The stories recorded in the Gospels state this faith. The first Christians certainly believed that on the third day after the Crucifixion, the tomb was empty and that Jesus appeared to them. There has been much discussion as to whether this was a bodily resurrection. For a discussion of the theories involved see Topic 25 of *The Gospels Today: An Approach to the Synoptic Gospels for GCSE* (by Eileen Bromley, published by Stanley Thornes).

Christians believe that they worship a living Lord, who has overcome the powers of evil and death and that it is possible for a believer to share in this new life. Here is one of the collects for Easter Day in the Anglican church:

> *Lord of all life and power,*
> *who through the mighty resurrection of*
>   *your Son*
> *overcame the old order of sin and death*
> *to make all things new in him:*
> *grant that we, being dead to sin*
> *and alive to you in Jesus Christ,*
> *may reign with him in glory;*
> *to whom with you and the Holy Spirit*
> *be praise and honour, glory and might,*
> *now and in all eternity.*
>
> The Alternative Service Book, 1980

ACTIVITIES

Lord Jesus Christ,
You have come to us,
You are one with us,
Mary's Son.
Cleansing our souls
From all their sin,
Pouring Your love
And goodness in,
Jesus, our love
For You we sing,
Living Lord.

Lord Jesus Christ,
You have come to us,
Born as one of us,
Mary's Son.
Led out to die
On Calvary,
Risen from death
To set us free,
Living Lord Jesus,
Help us see,
You are Lord.

Patrick Appleford

1 Read carefully these two verses of a modern hymn. Make a list of the Christian beliefs that are stated in them.

2 Use a hymn book to find a more traditional Easter hymn. Make notes of how the Gospel accounts are reflected in it.

3 Read again the collect for Easter Day. Then write in your own words what you think belief in the Resurrection can mean for a Christian.

4 Visit a church and make notes of any evidence you can find for the Christian belief in the Resurrection.

5 Discuss why you think the cross on the left has become a symbol of the Resurrection.

6 Discuss the following statements:

‘Jesus is dead: He died 2000 years ago.’

‘Jesus is alive: He is my Lord.’

How would holding either of these views affect an individual's attitude to life?

The Ascension and Return

He ascended into heaven and is seated at the right hand of the Father.
He will come again to judge the living and the dead.

The Apostles' Creed

Read **Mark** *13:24–7, 14:62, 16:19–20*
Luke *21:25–8, 22:69, 24:50–3*
Matthew *24:29–31, 25:1–46, 26:64*

After his resurrection, the Gospels suggest that Jesus appeared to his followers over a period of time (Acts 1:3 states that it was forty days). Then he left them, disappearing into a cloud. Clouds were symbols of the presence of God, so he had now returned to the Father.

The Ascension convinced the disciples that Jesus would not continue to appear to them in a physical form. As someone has suggested, Jesus had moved from one condition to another, rather than from one place to another. Ascension Day is always on a Thursday (forty days after

Easter) and is marked by special services in most churches. The following extract from a prayer is used as a preface to the Mass in Roman Catholic churches:

> *Father, all-powerful and ever-living God, we do well always and everywhere to give you thanks through Jesus Christ our Lord. In his risen body he plainly showed himself to his disciples and was taken up to heaven in their sight to claim for us a share in his divine life. And so, with all the choirs of angels in heaven we proclaim your glory . . .*
>
> *The Roman Missal*

Jesus had told his disciples that he would return to the world one day, 'in the clouds with great power and glory'.

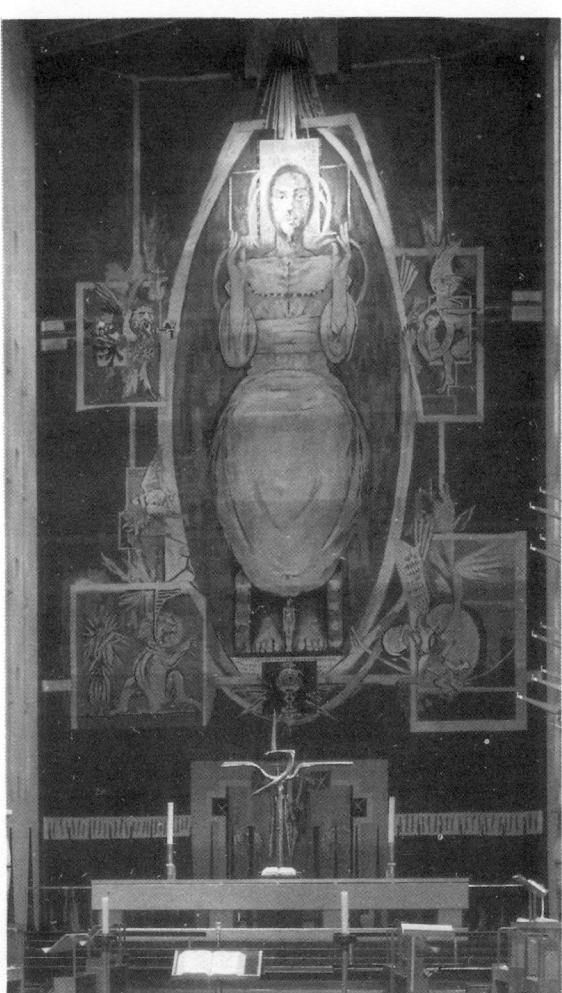

Graham Sutherland's tapestry, Christ in Glory, *in Coventry Cathedral*

The same symbolism is used as at the Ascension. Christians sometimes refer to this as the Second Coming, the Second Advent or the Return. Theologians use the Greek word *Parousia,* which means arrival. As the Apostles' Creed suggests, many Christians still expect the *Parousia* to occur at some point in the future. Jesus told a number of parables, encouraging people to be ready for it, and the judgement which would follow. Other Christians think that Jesus was referring to his coming again in the form of the Holy Spirit.

ACTIVITIES

1 Find a hymn about the Ascension. Discuss what it suggests about the significance of the event.

2 The Ascension has been described as a dramatic necessity to complete the story of the earthly life of Jesus. Discuss what this means.

3 'Jesus had moved from one condition to another, rather than from one place to another.' Discuss the symbolism of the Ascension.

4 Examine the photograph of Graham Sutherland's tapestry *Christ in Glory.* Write a paragraph on what it suggests to you.

5 'He will come again to judge the living and the dead.' Question a number of willing Christians on what they believe about:

   a) the return of Jesus
   b) judgement.

6 Produce some coursework to show how you would expect belief in each of the following to affect the behaviour of a Christian:

   a) the Incarnation
   b) the Atonement
   c) the Resurrection
   d) the Ascension
   e) the *Parousia*
   f) the Judgement.

   You could base some of your work on interviews or biographies of Christians.

The Holy Spirit

I believe in the Holy Spirit.

The Apostles' Creed

Read *Mark* 1:8, 10, 3:28–30
   Luke 1:15, 35, 41, 67, 3:22, 4:1, 14, 18, 10:21, 24:49
   Matthew 1:18–21, 3:11, 16, 4:1, 28:19

In parts of Britain Christians sometimes hold processions at Whitsuntide. They are celebrating the coming of the Holy Spirit. On the day of the Jewish feast of Pentecost, not long after the death and resurrection of Jesus, his followers had an amazing experience of the presence of the Spirit of God or the Spirit of Jesus with them (Acts 2:1–4). They had been told by Jesus to wait for this power to come upon them (Luke 24:49). Matthew records that they were also told to go and find disciples, baptising them 'in the name of the Father, the Son and the Holy Spirit'. From this, and other passages in the New Testament, grew up the doctrine of the Trinity (that one God exists in three persons).

The writers of the Gospels record that the Holy Spirit (the third person of the Trinity) was active before the birth of Jesus and played an important part in his life. It is stated that part of the message of John the Baptist was that Jesus would baptise people with the Holy Spirit.

This banner illustrates the Christian belief in the Holy Spirit

Early Christians believed in one almighty God, the Father, that they had met him in God the Son and continued to experience his presence and power through God the Holy Spirit.

ACTIVITIES

1

This symbol is sometimes used of the Trinity. Find any other suitable symbols to illustrate this belief.

2 Look again at the verses from the Gospels. Make a list of what the Gospels teach about the Holy Spirit.

3 Ask Christians what they understand by:
   a) the Holy Spirit
   b) the Trinity.
   Make notes of their replies.

4 Produce some coursework on the teaching about the Holy Spirit, in the Gospels, and in the Church today. To help you with the second part, use interviews, hymn-books and prayer-books.

5 Answer the following questions:

a) In which story is a dove mentioned in connection with Jesus?

b) What does the dove represent?

c) Suggest two reasons why the dove is an appropriate symbol on a Christmas card.

d) Give two examples of the way in which the Holy Spirit was active in the life of Jesus.

e) How do you think the Holy Spirit is active in the Church today?

A Christmas card sold in aid of the Leprosy Mission whose logo (Jesus touching a leprosy sufferer, Mark 1:40–2) appears on the left

The Church

I believe in . . . the holy catholic Church,
the communion of saints . . .

The Apostles' Creed

Read **Mark** *4:13–15*
Luke *22:17–20*
Matthew *16:13–20, 18:15–17, 28:19–20*

The Christian Church consists of very many denominations or groups, as do most of the religions of the world. It consists of people of all nations, who worship in small churches, large cathedrals, house groups or even in the open air.

What differences do you notice in the way these groups worship?

11

There are only two places in the Gospels where the word 'Church' is used. These are in two of the passages above, in Matthew's Gospel. The author of this Gospel seems to be particularly interested in the organisation of the early Church. However, because there is no mention of the Church in the other Gospels, it has been suggested that Jesus did not intend a Church to come into being. He certainly did not give details for an organisation, except to encourage the practice of baptism and sharing in the Lord's Supper. However, the fact that Jesus chose twelve apostles, with an inner group of three and a larger mission band of at least seventy suggests that he intended his followers to meet together in order to support each other, to meet with him and to take his message out to the world.

In the two thousand years since the time of Jesus, many denominations have come into existence with slightly different beliefs, mainly about authority and the organisation of the Church. The Apostles' Creed stresses the unity of all Christians throughout the world (the meaning of 'catholic Church'). Despite differences of practice, Christian believers are united in their faith in Jesus Christ.

Over the past fifty years, the ecumenical movement has encouraged Christians of all denominations to meet, pray, and work together and many inter-denominational groups and Churches exist today.

ACTIVITIES

1 Look up the following words in a dictionary and make a note of the meaning of each: holy, catholic, Church, communion, saint, denomination, ecumenical.

2 Make a list of the instructions that Jesus gave about the Church.

3 Answer the following questions:
  a) What is the meaning of ecumenical (from the Greek word *oikoumene*)?

  b) What two activities did Jesus tell his disciples to carry out in the future?
  c) This symbol (see also the photograph on page 49) is that of the World Council of Churches. What do you think is its significance?
  d) What do you think is meant by 'the communion of saints'?
  e) Do you think Jesus intended a Church to come into being?

4 Find out which Christian denominations are represented in your area. Discover if there is a local council of Churches and what ecumenical activities take place.

5 ‘I attend St Peter's Church.’

  ‘I am a Christian, but see no need to attend a Church.’

  ‘I am a Catholic.’

  ‘I am a member of the Catholic Church and worship in a house group.’

  Discuss the differences between these statements.

6 If there is a Christian Union or similar inter-denominational group in your school, interview those who attend to find out what they have in common.

Forgiveness of Sins

I believe in . . . the forgiveness of sins.

The Apostles' Creed

. . . for our salvation, he came down from heaven.

Nicene Creed

Read *Mark* 1:1–5, 2:1–17
Luke 1:67–79, 2:29–32, 3:3–6, 7:41–50, 11:4, 15:11–32, 17:3–4, 19:1–10
Matthew 6:12–15, 18:21–35

A favourite theme in Luke's Gospel is that of salvation. He introduces the theme near the start of the Gospel, where the words of Zechariah concerning his new-born son are:

> **You will go ahead of the Lord**
> **to prepare his road for him,**
> **to tell his people that they will be saved**
> **by having their sins forgiven.**
>
> Luke 1:76–7

We use the verb 'to save' more frequently than the noun 'salvation'. We have all heard of people being saved from dangerous situations and even from death.

The *Concise Oxford Dictionary* has this definition of salvation:

> **Saving of the soul; deliverance from sin and its consequences and admission to heaven brought about by Christ.**

The parables of the lost, especially that of the Lost Son, suggest the possibility of forgiveness for those who repent. John the Baptist preached about the forgiveness of sins for those who are repentant. Part of the Lord's Prayer is a request for forgiveness. Prayers of penitence have always been important for individual Christians, and have played an important part in the worship of the Church, particularly in the service of Holy Communion, for instance:

> **Almighty God, our heavenly Father,**
> **we have sinned against you and against**
> **our fellow men,**
> **in thought and word and deed,**
> **through negligence, through weakness,**
> **through our own deliberate fault.**
> **We are truly sorry,**
> **and repent of all our sins.**
> **For the sake of your Son Jesus Christ,**
> **who died for us,**
> **forgive us all that is past;**
> **and grant that we may serve you in**
> **newness of life**
> **to the glory of your name. Amen.**
>
> *The Alternative Service Book*, 1980

13

ACTIVITIES

1 If you are studying Luke's Gospel, list what he says about:

a) salvation

b) the forgiveness of sins.

2

> • . . . *he has set them free*
> • . . . *a mighty Saviour*
> • . . . *the bright dawn of salvation . . .*
> • *All mankind will see God's salvation*
> • *Forgive us . . . as we forgive . . .*
> • *Your sins are forgiven*

Answer the following questions:

a) Give examples of two people who were told 'Your sins are forgiven'.

b) What did John the Baptist say about forgiveness?

c) What connection is made in the Gospels between divine and human forgiveness?

d) What teaching is there in the parable of the Lost Son on forgiveness?

e) What do you think is the Christian teaching about salvation?

3 Discuss the connection between salvation and the forgiveness of sins.

4 Use any Christian prayer books to find further examples of prayers of penitence.

Life after Death

*I believe in . . . the resurrection of the body
and the life everlasting.*

The Apostles' Creed

Read   *Mark* 5:35–43, 12:18–27
          Luke 8:49–56, 20:27–40
          Matthew 7:13–14, 9:18:26, 22:23–33

> • *Death is the greatest fact of life*
> • *Death is the end*
> • *Death will be my birthday . . .*
>   Richard Sibbes
> • *Death is the foreshadowing of life. We die that we may die no more.*
>   Thomas Hooker
> • *After death – nothing*
> • *At death we leave behind all we have and take with us all we are.*
> • *Death for the Christian is not a miserable cul-de-sac, but a glorious open road into the presence of God.*
>   D. Barnett

A book has been written called *The Last Thing We Talk About* (Joseph Bayly, Scripture Union, 1970). Three sons of the author had died, but despite his sorrow he felt it important to write about his conviction that death is not the end. The subject of death is often considered to be a morbid one, but Christianity has very positive teaching on the subject. Think about the opposite list of statements made on the subject of death.

There are hints in the Gospels of Jesus' teaching about life after death. As well as a reply he gave to people who asked him about life after death, he also taught on the subject when he raised people who had died. The resurrection of

What does this suggest about Christian beliefs in life after death?

Jesus is central to the Christian belief in life after death. We have already considered the importance of this in Topic 5.

The Christian belief that death is a new beginning rather than the end of life is often expressed in the inscriptions on gravestones, as in the picture above.

Here is a prayer sometimes used at a funeral service which gives comfort in the belief that death is not the end of life.

> *. . . And now we give thee thanks, because through him [Jesus Christ] thou hast given us the hope of a glorious resurrection, so that although death comes to us all, yet we rejoice in the promise of eternal life; for to thy faithful people life is changed, not taken away, and when our mortal flesh is laid aside, an everlasting dwelling place is made ready for us in heaven.*
>
> *The Alternative Service Book,* 1980

ACTIVITIES

1 'The last thing we talk about'. It is sometimes suggested that death is one of the few subjects rarely discussed these days. Discuss whether this is so in your experience.

2 Look at the inscriptions on gravestones or monuments in a church yard or cemetery and at announcements of deaths in newspapers. List any Christian beliefs that are expressed in them.

3 Try to find a funeral service in a Christian prayer book. Write a paragraph on the teaching about death that it contains.

4 'Be sure to celebrate my funeral . . . It is a better day than one's wedding day' (C.T. Studd). Why do you think a Christian might wish to hold a celebration rather than a morbid ceremony?

5 Look up Mark 5:35–43, Luke 8:49–56 or Matthew 9:18–26 and answer the following questions:
   a) What do you know about the person who, according to this account, had died?
   b) Mention two other occasions when Jesus raised someone from death.
   c) What does the passage suggest about Jesus' attitude to death?
   d) 'Death will be my birthday.' What is your opinion about the attitude expressed in this statement?

Section B RESPONSES

Faith

Read *Mark* 2:5, 5:25–36, 6:5–6, 9:14–29, 10:46–52, 11:20–4
Luke 5:20, 7:1–10, 48–50, 17:5–6, 11–19, 18:35–43
Matthew 8:5–13, 9:1–2, 20–2, 15:21–8

In the first section of the book we considered some statements of Christian belief. In each case, a quotation from the Apostles' Creed introduced the belief. A creed, from the Latin word *credo* meaning 'I believe', is a statement of such beliefs. Sometimes the term 'the Christian faith' is given to such a statement of beliefs. However, the word 'faith' usually means more than a belief in the mind. It can also mean an act of trust.

The Gospels suggest that Jesus encouraged people to respond to him in the sense of putting their whole trust in him, and acting upon their beliefs. A number of miracles are recorded in such a way that they emphasise the importance

of faith in Jesus' power to heal, and the words '... your faith has made you well' are often used. Jesus commended people for their faith, both Jews and Gentiles, as well as rebuking others for a lack of faith. When Jesus visited his home town of Nazareth, we are told that he was unable to perform many miracles because 'the people did not have faith'.

Jesus also encouraged his disciples to live by faith, or trust in God, rather than worrying about material things. You may have heard of the schoolboy's remark that faith is believing what you know is not true! In the Gospels, faith means a trust and commitment which changes an individual's life.

A visitor on a youth exchange to Benin needed to trust another person in order to cross this swamp

ACTIVITIES

1 Look up the word 'faith' in as many dictionaries as you can find. Discuss the different meanings of the word.

2 Carry out a survey to discover what people understand by the word 'faith'. Present the results as a list or chart.

3 Answer each of the following questions, briefly:

a) Name two people who were told by Jesus '. . . your faith has made you well'.

b) Where was Jesus unable to perform miracles because of an absence of faith?

c) Give an example of a Gentile whose faith was commended.

d) When were Jesus' disciples rebuked for their lack of faith?

e) Who was told 'Everything is possible for the person who has faith'?

f) Who was encouraged, 'Don't be afraid, only believe'?

4 Answer each part of the following question in an essay:

a) Describe an occasion recorded in the Gospels when a person's faith was commended.

b) Explain how the miracles are used in the Gospels to teach about faith.

c) Explain the meaning of the word 'faith' as it is used in the Gospels.

d) What do you think people today mean by faith?

5 Discuss any examples you know of people who have shown the kind of faith spoken of in the Gospels.

6 Look again at the photograph opposite. What does it suggest about the meaning of trust?

Baptism

Read *Mark* 1:1–11
Luke 3:1–22
Matthew 3:1–17, 28:19–20

Two of the reasons why the Christian Church today practises baptism are that Jesus was himself baptised and, at the end of his Gospel, Matthew suggests that Jesus gave a command about baptism at the close of his ministry on earth. Baptism is seen as both a symbolic act and as a sacrament (a means of transmitting God's grace or undeserved favour). Some, including the Roman Catholic Church and the Anglican Church, baptise infants and adults by sprinkling with water. Some Christian groups have a service of dedication for babies and baptise adults by total immersion when they wish to make a public witness to their faith. This is often called 'believers' baptism' and is practised, for example, in Baptist churches. The United Reformed Church now recognises both infant and believers' baptism.

'Twin track' baptism is here to stay

INFANT baptism and believers' baptism were re-affirmed at the United Reformed Church's annual assembly.

The 'twin track' policy – because it is a union of Congregational and Presbyterian churches which practise infant baptism and the Churches of Christ which practise believers' baptism – was debated as the denomination sought to discourage re-baptism in some of its churches. The debate also revealed the need for a suitable adult rite of confirmation.

Katy is baptised by her grandfather in an Anglican church

Rose is baptised by her father in a Baptist church

A prayer used at an Anglican baptism emphasises the symbolism of water:

> **Almighty God, whose Son Jesus Christ was baptised in the river Jordan; we thank you for the gift of water to cleanse us and revive us; we thank you that through the waters of the Red Sea, you led your people out of slavery to freedom in the promised land; we thank you that through the deep waters of death you brought your Son, and raised him to life in triumph. Bless this water, that your servants who are washed in it may be made one with Christ in his death and in his resurrection, to be cleansed and delivered from all sin.**
>
> **Send your Holy Spirit upon them to bring them to new birth in the family of your Church, and raise them with Christ to full and eternal life.**
>
> *The Alternative Service Book, 1980*

A Baptist minister describes a baptismal service:

> **Before the baptism, candidates are given an opportunity to give a testimony to their faith in Jesus Christ, if they wish to do so. There is a baptistry at the front of the church which is normally covered. I enter the water, followed by the candidate. I ask two questions, 'Do you confess with your mouth and believe in your heart that Jesus Christ is Saviour and Lord?' and 'Do you promise that, God helping you, you will walk in the ways of Christ all the days of your life?' I then say, 'I gladly baptise you in the name of the Father, and of the Son, and of the Holy Spirit'. The candidate is briefly immersed under the water and then leaves the pool by the other steps to symbolise that they are one with Christ in his death and resurrection.**

ACTIVITIES

1 If any members of the group have attended an infant baptism or a believer's baptism, describe it to everyone.

2 If you are able to visit a church which practises infant baptism, look for the font and find out what is important about its position.

3 If you have contact with a Baptist minister, ask if you can visit the church and see the baptistry. The minister might explain to you what happens at a baptism.

4 Looking again at the photographs and quotations, answer the following questions:

a) Give two reasons why Christians practise baptism.

b) Explain what is meant by a sacrament.

c) What Biblical events are referred to in the Anglican prayer?

d) Why is an adult completely immersed at a believers' baptism?

e) What are the main differences between infant and believers' baptism?

Holy Communion

Read *Mark* 14:22–6
      Luke 22:14–23
      Matthew 26:26–30

Holy Communion is considered by most churches to be the central act of Christian worship, and had its origins in the Last Supper. The celebration is known by various names: the Eucharist, the Mass, Holy Communion, the Lord's Supper, the Breaking of Bread.

This is one of the very few issues in the Gospels where there is a difference of belief between the Christian denominations. Roman Catholics believe that the body and blood of Jesus are present on the altar in the bread and wine, a doctrine known as transubstantiation:

> *At Mass, through the ministry of his earthly priests, Jesus Christ becomes truly, really and substantially present on the altar under the appearances of bread and of wine: and re-presents Himself to God the Father on behalf of the human race.*
>
> Catholic Truth Society

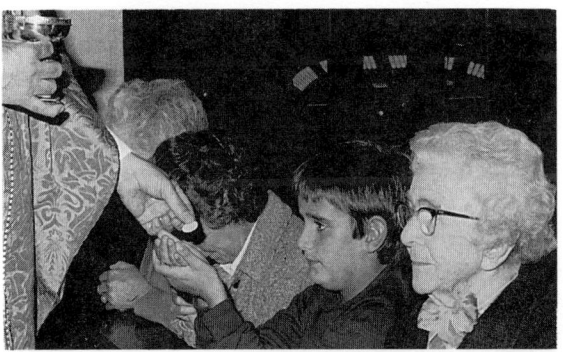
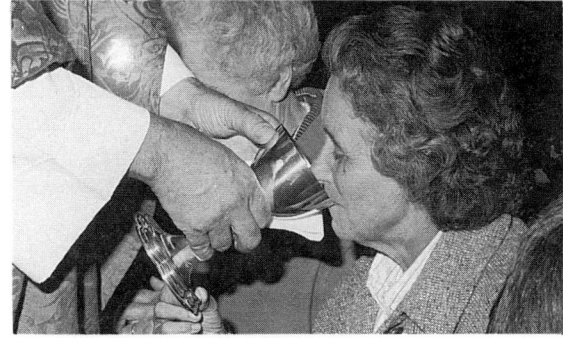

Celebrations of Holy Communion

19

Most Protestants would consider that the bread and wine are symbols or reminders of the body and blood of Jesus. The vast majority of Christians believe that it is important to obey the command of Luke 22:19, 'Do this in memory of me'.

There are a number of different ways of observing this celebration, but all who participate in it agree that it is an important spiritual experience. A prayer used in a number of churches shows the importance of the Christian's attitude when participating in this celebration:

> *Lord, we come to your table trusting in your mercy and not in any goodness of our own. We are not worthy even to gather up the crumbs under your table, but it is your nature always to have mercy, and on that we depend. So feed us with the body and blood of Jesus Christ, your Son, that we may forever live in him and he in us. Amen.*
>
> *Methodist Service Book*

ACTIVITIES

1 Try to discover the meaning and significance of the various names used for this celebration.

2 If any member of your group has attended a service of Holy Communion, describe it to the other members of the class.

3 Talk to any Christians you know about the celebration of Holy Communion in their church. Find out the name used for the service, how often it is held, who is allowed to take part, and what happens. Make a class chart to show your findings.

4 Look at as many prayer and service books of different churches as you can find. Write a paragraph to show how the celebration of Holy Communion today is based on the Gospel accounts you have studied.

5 The Last Supper was a celebration of the *Seder*, the Jewish Passover meal. If you have a copy of *The Gospels: A GCSE Activities Pack*, (Eileen Bromley, Stanley Thornes) or the similar pack on *Judaism*, use the activity sheet on the *Seder* to share a celebration together.

Sunday Worship

TOPIC 14

Read *Mark* 2:23–3:6
Luke 4:16, 6:1–11

There is almost as much controversy today concerning the observance of Sunday as there was about Sabbath observance at the time of Jesus. Over the past few years there have been attempts to change the Sunday trading laws, and a 'Keep Sunday Special' campaign has had considerable support. By the time the Gospels were written, Christians were keeping the first day of the week as their day of rest and worship. This was known as 'the Lord's Day' as it was the day on which Jesus rose from the dead. So, whereas Jews celebrate the seventh day, Saturday, as the Sabbath, most Christians observe Sunday as their day for worship. However, one group, the Seventh-Day Adventists, believe that Saturday should still be observed:

> *The Sabbath is the seventh day of the week.*
>
> *Adventists believe that both Old and New Testaments teach the sacredness of the seventh day, a memorial to God's creative power and a recognition of His authority. Adventists observe the Sabbath from sunset Friday to sunset Saturday, in harmony with the fourth commandment of the Decalogue.*
>
> A Brief Introduction to Seventh-Day Adventists

Christians remember that Jesus worshipped regularly in the synagogue. Many feel a need to meet with others to worship, to learn about their faith and to share in Christian activities together.

These Christians find worship a joyful experience

ACTIVITIES

1 Read the following letter written to a daily newspaper. Discuss it. Do you think the points it makes are valid?

Keep Sunday special

SIR – The traditional and special nature of Sunday is once again under threat (. . .) from commercial pressure to remove all restrictions on Sunday trading and the Sunday Sport Bill, sponsored by Andrew MacKay MP.

If all restrictions are removed, Sunday as we know it will be a thing of the past. There is need for reform but there are ways of doing this without total deregulation. It is argued that in a free society everyone should be free to shop and engage in sport if they wish. However, a full programme of sport, and unrestricted trading will deprive millions of their freedom to enjoy Sunday as a day of rest. Sunday is special and should remain so. A day of rest is part of God's will and purpose for people and keeping Sunday special provides the opportunity for families to enjoy rest and recreation together. Family life is important and is placed at risk if Sunday becomes as any other day.

Those on low incomes will have very little power or influence to protect their Sunday and will almost certainly lose their right of choice. Many will be prevented from attending services of worship. Sunday kept special also serves as a sign and symbol of Christ's resurrection and our acknowledgement of God's place in our nation's life.

2 Do you think it is necessary to have one day in seven for rest and worship? Does it matter which day? Write a paragraph expressing your opinion.

Do you think the Christian view is the same as or different from yours? Add a note about this.

3 If you have people from different Christian Churches in your group, ask them to give a brief description of the worship of their Church.

4 Look at church notice boards in your area. Make a note of the activities that take place on Sundays. List them under three headings: Worship, Christian education and Christian fellowship.

5
> *The Sabbath was made for the good of man; man was not made for the Sabbath.*
>
> Mark 2:27

Discuss the meaning of these words.

6 Produce some coursework on Sunday observance, or Sunday worship. Use information that you have found in the Gospels, in this Topic and by talking to Christians. Collect cuttings from newspapers and magazines (especially church magazines) to illustrate your work.

7 If you are able to do so, attend Sunday worship in at least two different church denominations. Write a comparison of the worship.

Discipleship

Read *Mark* 1:14–20, 2:13–17, 8:34–8, 10:17:31
Luke 5:1–11, 27–32, 9:57–62, 14:25–35
Matthew 4:18–22, 9:9–13

❝I follow the teaching of the Buddha.❞

❝I am a disciple of Confucius.❞

❝I am a disciple of Jesus.❞

❝I follow Marx.❞

As the above examples show, a disciple is someone who learns from another; so at some point in life, most of us have been 'disciples'. For a follower of Jesus, discipleship involves life-long L-plates:

Parallels are often drawn between the call of the first disciples and people becoming followers of Jesus today. Mark 1:14–20 is often read at confirmations in the Church of England, and the following questions and responses are used in a Methodist service when an adult is to be both baptised and confirmed:

Minister	*You have heard Jesus saying to you, as he said to his first disciples, Follow me. You have already responded to his call, and you sincerely desire to be saved from your sins through faith in him. I ask you therefore: Do you repent of your sins and renounce all evil?*
Answer	*I do.*
Minister	*Do you trust in Jesus Christ as your Lord and Saviour?*
Answer	*I do.*
Minister	*Will you obey Christ and serve him in the Church and in the world?*
Answer	*With his help I will.*

Methodist Service Book

Jesus discouraged some would-be followers, pointing out to them that discipleship is not easy. Christian commitment today is also costly.

ACTIVITIES

1 Consider the questions and responses from the Methodist service. Write down two separate parts of it which reflect teaching from the Gospels.

2 Collect any examples you can find of people who have given up their jobs in order to 'catch men'. Church and missionary magazines might help you to find examples.

3 Jesus taught what Christian discipleship would involve. Make a list of the points he made about discipleship.

4

> *Whoever wants to save his own life will lose it; but whoever loses his life for my sake will save it.*

Discuss the meaning of these words.

5 Look up Mark 8:34, Luke 9:23 or Matthew 16:24. These verses suggest that a Christian should take discipleship very seriously. Write down what effects this might have on the way a Christian lives.

6 Prepare a meditation on the subject of discipleship. Include readings, hymns and prayers.

Pilgrimage   TOPIC 16

Read *Mark* 9:30–41, 10:32–45
Luke 9:43–56, 18:31–4
Matthew 17:22–3, 20:17–19

Jews who were able to do so were expected to visit the Temple in Jerusalem three times a year for the great pilgrim festivals: Passover, Pentecost and Tabernacles. The passages above record a journey made to Jerusalem by Jesus and his followers for the Passover festival. This journey was to end with the arrest, trial and crucifixion of Jesus. The followers of Jesus were also learning that discipleship is a pilgrimage, a process of learning.

People still make pilgrimages, especially to the Holy Land. There they might spend time in meditation and prayer at the possible sites of events in the life of Jesus. For instance, on Good Friday, pilgrims might follow the Via Dolorosa (the Way of Sorrows), some perhaps carrying a cross as Jesus did to his crucifixion, and pausing to think and pray at each of the stations of the cross.

Other places of pilgrimage might be connected with important events or people in the history of Christianity, for instance, Canterbury and Lourdes. Sometimes pilgrimages are made to particular churches or other places in order to attend conferences or meetings for worship, for example to Taizé in France or Iona in Scotland.

One Christian denomination recently organised a series of pilgrim walks in order to focus attention on the importance of prayer.

PILGRIMS

YOUR OPPORTUNITY TO MAKE A PERSONAL PILGRIMAGE WITH A SUPPORTIVE GROUP OF FRIENDS.

In this noisy hi-tech society many of us find it hard to pray. We often feel that we're hopeless at prayer and that we've failed in the Christian life. PILGRIMS will stimulate you to pray and give a basic introduction to various kinds of prayer. But it won't be boring... it'll be more fun than a hike!

ACTIVITIES

1 Make a list of places which might be visited by Christian pilgrims today. Make a note of the event or person associated with each site, and any other reasons for their significance.

2 Find out about any pilgrimages that Christians might make today. Discover the purpose of the pilgrimage for the individual. Notice that not all Christians believe that it is important to make such journeys.

3 Produce an illustrated diary of a Christian pilgrimage to a place of your choice. Collect illustrations (travel brochures might help), and show the effect such a journey might have on a pilgrim.

4 Try to find a copy of Chaucer's *Canterbury Tales.* You will not find it easy to read, but try to discover when it was written and what it describes.

5 Try to find a copy of either John Bunyan's *Pilgrim's Progress,* or of the hymn taken from the book, 'Who would true valour see . . .' Discuss the idea of pilgrimage in the hymn.

6

> *Jesus . . . set out on his way to Jerusalem*

Answer the following questions:

a) For which festival was Jesus going to Jerusalem?

b) For which other two festivals did Jews also try to visit the Temple?

c) What dangers would Jesus face in Jerusalem?

d) Why do you think some people go on pilgrimages today?

e) What do you think is meant by the phrase 'discipleship is a pilgrimage'?

7

> **Pilgrimage Prayer**
>
> *O Lord Jesus Christ, yourself the way, the truth and the life; Grant to us who shall tread in your earthly footsteps, a sense of awe, wonder and holiness. May our hearts burn within us as we come to know you more clearly, love you more dearly and follow you more nearly. Amen*

Discuss what is suggested about pilgrimage in this prayer.

Prayer

Read *Mark* 1:35, 6:41, 46, 8:6, 11:20–5, 14:32–6, 15:34
Luke 6:12–13, 10:21–2, 11:1–13, 18:1–14, 22:31–2, 39–46, 23:34, 46, 24:30
Matthew 5:23–4, 6:5–15, 7:7 11, 18:15 20, 26:36–9

'For me, prayer is a daily habit.'

'I do not believe in God, so there is no point in praying.'

'Prayer is talking to God.'

'I pray when I am in trouble.'

'I pray only when I go to church, and that is not often.'

'Prayer is like picking up the telephone and having a conversation with God.'

These statements about prayer reflect people's beliefs about God. Not only in the teaching of Jesus, but throughout the Bible there are commands and encouragements to pray. If, as Jesus taught, there is an almighty God who has reached out to human beings in his Son, and with whom it is possible for an individual to have a relationship, then private, devotional prayer is a privilege rather than a duty for a Christian. The Christian community has also believed, through the centuries, that corporate prayer (praying together) is an essential part of worship.

Prayer is much more than making requests. Some Christians find the use of an acrostic a convenient way of remembering the different aspects of prayer. One acrostic is on the word ACTS:

Adoration	praising
Confession	saying sorry
Thanksgiving	thanking
Supplication	asking

ACTIVITIES

1 Consider the Lord's Prayer and make a note of which parts of it fit into the sections of the acrostic on ACTS.

2 Use the subject index at the back of this book to find prayers that have been included. Choose two of them and show how they fit into the pattern of the ACTS acrostic.

3 Try to obtain a prayer book or service book of one of the Christian Churches. Make a list of some of the occasions when a congregation would join in corporate prayer.

4 Read Mark 14:32–6, Luke 22:39–44 or Matthew 26:36–9 and answer the following questions:
   a) What is meant by 'this cup of suffering'?
   b) What request was made in this prayer?
   c) Describe briefly another occasion when Jesus prayed.

   d) What does the above passage suggest about the problem of un-answered prayer?
   e) What do you think a Christian might learn about prayer from this passage?

5   ‘To pray is to use God as a heavenly Father Christmas.’

   ‘Prayer is more than asking God to run errands for us.’

   ‘Prayer is not persuading God to do what we want: it is bringing ourselves in line with what he wants.’

   ‘Prayer is the enjoyment of the presence of God.’

   Discuss the above comments, in the light of Jesus' teaching about prayer and his practice of it.

6 Discuss the statements made at the start of this Topic. How do they reflect differing beliefs about God?

7 Carry out a survey of a willing group of Christians about their practice of prayer. Make sure that any replies remain anonymous.

Stewardship

Read *Mark* 12:41–4
  Luke 12:31–8, 41–8, 16:1–17, 19:11–27, 21:1–4
  Matthew 24:45–51, 25:14–30

Christians see in these passages an encouragement to stewardship; to see everything they have as a trust from God, to be used in serving him. So time, talents and material possessions are all seen as part of their stewardship.

This idea has been stressed throughout the history of the Church, but during the last thirty years it has become common for churches of various denominations to organise Stewardship Campaigns amongst their members. These encourage Christians to see their time, talents and gifts as a trust from God, to be used in the service of Jesus Christ. This response is summed up in the following prayer:

> *Lord Jesus Christ, you have taught us that we cannot love God and money, and that all our possessions are a trust from you. Teach us to be faithful stewards of our time, our talents and our money, and that we may help others and extend your kingdom; for your name's sake. Amen*
>
> M.H. Botting

The teaching of Jesus demanded a response, as we have seen in Topic 15 on Discipleship. In the parables, especially those recorded by Luke, Jesus frequently likened his followers to servants or stewards of a master. Their use, or abuse, of property committed to them by the master is a recurring theme in these parables.

Those involved in a Stewardship Campaign are encouraged to make pledges concerning their use of time, talents and possessions:

WHAT IS CHRISTIAN STEWARDSHIP?

AS Christians we believe that everything we have – our health, wealth, time and talents – are gifts from God entrusted to us. To some he has given skills in making and mending; to some the ability to use their minds in many directions; to others the ability to listen to those in need, to give time to those who need company; to others . . .

We are called to offer back to God the talents he has given us. That is what Christian Stewardship is about.

Christian Stewardship is an opportunity for each one of us to sit down and carefully assess how we are to use all that God has given us, and how we can best express our discipleship in and through the Church.

It challenges us to respond realistically to the claims that Jesus Christ makes on our lives, *our time, talents* and *money.*

ACTIVITIES

1 Collect any information that you can find about Stewardship Campaigns. Church members may be able to help you.

2 Discuss the advantages and disadvantages of this approach to Christian stewardship.

3 Look up the following words in a dictionary and make a note of their meaning: steward, service, talent, commitment, campaign, materialism.

4 Consider carefully the above information about Christian Stewardship. Show how a Christian's life might be affected if he/she participated in such a campaign. List your points under three headings:

Time	Talents	Possessions

5 ❮ It's mine: I'll do what I like with it. ❯
❮ It's a trust from God: I'll use it to help other people. ❯

Discuss these two attitudes to money. Can you suggest other attitudes that people have to their possessions?

6 Read Luke 19:11–27 or Matthew 25:14–30 and answer the following questions:

a) Which servants were commended by the master?

b) Which servant was criticised by the master?

c) Why was the servant criticised?

d) What does the parable teach about Stewardship?

e) What is your opinion about Church Stewardship campaigns?

7

> *. . . to every person who has something, even more will be given . . . but the person who has nothing, even the little that he has will be taken away from him*
>
> Luke 19:26, Matthew 25:29

Discuss this verse as a comment on stewardship.

8 Look again at the Responses in this section of the book. Discuss whether you think they would all be appropriate for all Christians.

Advent

Read *Luke* 1:5–80
Mark 13:1–27

Although the celebration of Advent was not introduced into the Christian Church until about the Sixth century, many aspects of it have their origins in the Gospels.

Advent means 'coming' and during a period of roughly a month before Christmas, many Christians prepare for the coming of Jesus Christ. Advent includes the four Sundays before Christmas day, and is the start of the Christian year. It is intended to be a time for thought and preparation and it is sometimes called a 'penitential season', a time for repentance or being sorry for sins. Passages from the Gospels read during Advent include the birth of John the Baptist and the Annunciation to Mary. Christians also look forward to the 'second Advent' or the return of Jesus Christ to the world as a King, rather than as an infant. This Christian doctrine is sometimes known as the *Parousia* (see Topic 6). Themes stressed during Advent are therefore: preparation, repentance, judgement and salvation. For most children, however, Advent is a time of increasing excitement as Christmas approaches.

You may have seen Advent calendars, or an

Advent wreath with five candles, one being lit for each of the four Sundays of Advent and one on Christmas Day. There are special Advent hymns and sometimes Advent carol services are held in churches. The following prayers are used in some churches on the two Sundays before Christmas:

The Forerunner

Almighty God, who sent your servant John the Baptist to prepare your people for the coming of your Son: inspire the ministers and stewards of your truth to turn our disobedient hearts to the law of love; that when he comes again in glory, we may stand with confidence before him as our judge; who is alive and reigns with you and the Holy Spirit, one God, now and for ever.

Collect for Advent 3

The Annunciation

Heavenly Father, who chose the Virgin Mary to be the mother of our Lord and Saviour; fill us with your grace, that in all things we may accept your holy will and with her rejoice in your salvation; through Jesus Christ our Lord.

Collect for Advent 4
The Methodist Service Book

ACTIVITIES

1 Compare the two prayers in this topic with the passages which you have read in the Gospels. Write down any connections you notice.

2 Ask Christians what they understand Advent to mean and how it is observed. Make notes of their replies.

3 Look up again Luke 1:68–79 and answer the following questions:

a) According to the tradition of the Gospels, after which event were these words first spoken?

b) In what ways would the child (v.76) prepare the way for the Lord?

c) Which themes, stressed during Advent, are to be found in this passage?

d) Why do you think this passage is often read in churches during Advent?

4 Find a copy of 'O come, O come, Immanuel', or another Advent hymn, and write a paragraph to explain its connection with the Gospels.

5 Working in a group, make an Advent calendar, with appropriate Biblical texts and symbols or illustrations.

Christmas

TOPIC 20

Read *Luke* 2:1–20
Matthew 1:18–25

The date of Jesus' birth is unknown, and was probably not 25 December, but the festival has been celebrated on this date by the Church in Western Europe since the Fourth century. Christmas is probably the best known and most popular Christian festival, although not the most important. It is based upon the Christian belief that God became man in Jesus (see Topic 2). The passages above are frequently used in church services. There are special carol services, and midnight services of Holy Communion (called Mass in the Catholic Church) on Christmas Eve. Nativity plays are frequently performed by both children and adults, and families mark the festival with special meals and parties.

Over the centuries many traditions and customs have been added to the festival from various parts of the world. Some customs have more connection with pagan festivities than with Christianity. The festival has also become very commercialised, with Christmas goods appearing in the shops earlier each year.

Christmas values have gone

DEAR EDITOR,

Well, it's over. Thank goodness.

Christmas and the New Year is getting worse each time it comes around.

It gets more expensive, more commercialised and less the Church festival it is meant to be.

And I'm sure in a few years we'll be seeing shops opening on Christmas Day itself – as if a few don't already! – and sales starting mid-December.

The youngsters of today are not taught about Christmas and its meaning. Surely television could play a larger part in this.

I noticed Christmas Day viewing from start to finish was virtually all based on entertainment value and not the Christian message.

I am not a regular church-goer, in fact I only go to church for christenings, marriages and funerals, but I miss the Christian connection, linking the festivities with the birth of Jesus.

ACTIVITIES

1 Look up again Luke 2:15–20 and answer the following questions:

   a) Why, according to Luke, did the shepherds decide to go to Bethlehem?

   b) What had the shepherds been told?

   c) What Christian belief is the celebration of Christmas based on?

   d) What would you consider to be an ideal Christian celebration of Christmas?

2 Make a list of Christmas customs. Add comments about their origins: whether they are connected with the Gospel accounts or with pre-Christian customs, and which country they come from.

3 Some Christians believe that Christmas has become too commercialised. Read again the above letter to a newspaper and discuss your opinions about this.

4 Work out a Christmas meditation or service for an assembly, including readings and carols. Perhaps you could present it?

5 Find a Christmas carol which is closely related to Luke 2:1–20. Discuss whether any additional legendary material has been added to the statements made in the passage.

6 Some groups do not celebrate Christmas because of the impossibility of knowing the actual date of Jesus' birth, the pagan customs involved, or the commercialisation of the festival. Discuss your opinions about this.

Epiphany

Read *Matthew* 2:1–12, 3:13–17

The story of the visit of the wise men to the infant Jesus is often incorporated into the Christmas celebrations, especially into nativity plays. However, some churches celebrate this event at Epiphany, on 6 January. Epiphany means 'showing' or 'manifestation' and it celebrates the showing of the child Jesus to the wise men, who represent the nations of the world. Light is an important symbol at this time, and this has been emphasised by many Christian artists, as here, in this painting by the Sixteenth century Italian artist Paolo Veronese, called *The Adoration of the Kings,* in the National Gallery in London.

A Church of England collect for Epiphany is:

Eternal God, who by the shining of a star led the wise men to the worship of your Son: guide by his light the nations of the earth, that the whole world may behold your glory; through Jesus Christ our Lord.

The Alternative Service Book, 1980

It is interesting that a special service is still held at which gold, frankincense and myrrh are presented on behalf of the Queen.

However, in some Eastern Orthodox churches, Epiphany celebrates the showing of Jesus to the public at the time of his baptism, and so the passage from Matthew 3 is read.

ACTIVITIES

1 Try to find a list of Christian seasons and festivals. There is often one in prayer books and service books and sometimes in diaries. Make a list of those festivals which you expect to have connections with the Gospels. As you continue with the course, add the references from the Gospels to your list.

2 Look at a service book or prayer book (you will find these in various churches) and make a note of the way in which any of the passages you have studied already are used in church worship.

3 Look up again Matthew 2:1–12 and answer the following questions:

a) What is the name of the Christian festival which is based on this story?

b) Explain why this name is sometimes used.

c) Which other event in the life of Jesus is celebrated by some Christians at this festival?

d) What is the connection between the two stories?

e) Why do you think that light is such an important symbol at this festival?

4 Ask any Christians you may know whether they celebrate Epiphany. Make a list of their replies and which churches they may have a connection with. What does this show you about practices in different denominations (branches of the Church)?

Lent

Read *Mark* 1:12–13
      Luke 4:1–13
      Matthew 4:1–11

You may have heard the question asked, 'What are you giving up for Lent?' Lent is not a festival, but a fast; in some ways a 'penitential season' similar to Advent. It is a period of roughly forty days leading up to the major Christian festival of Easter. It was probably first observed in the Fourth century AD and is a period of self-denial intended to remind Christians of Jesus' period of fasting and temptation in the desert. It is immediately preceded by Shrove Tuesday, and the first day of Lent is known as Ash Wednesday. Both of these names suggest practices which are still observed by some churches.

The significance of Lent is emphasised in this preface to the Roman Catholic Mass for the first Sunday of Lent.

> *Father, all-powerful and ever-living God, we do well always and everywhere to give you thanks through Jesus Christ our Lord. His fast of forty days makes this a holy season of self-denial. By rejecting the devil's temptations he has taught us to rid ourselves of the hidden corruption of evil, and so to share his paschal meal in purity of heart, until we come to its fulfilment in the promised land of heaven.*
>
> *The Roman Missal*

ACTIVITIES

1

> *And now we give you thanks because through him [Jesus] you have given us the spirit of discipline, that we may triumph over evil and grow in grace.*
>
> *The Alternative Service Book, 1980*

The above quotation is a preface used at Holy Communion during Lent. Answer the following questions:

a) How did Jesus 'triumph over evil'?
b) What events in the Gospels are commemorated during Lent?
c) How long is Lent observed for, and why?
d) What is the significance of 'discipline' during Lent?
e) How appropriate do you consider the above prayer to be for a service held during Lent?

2 Mothering Sunday is observed on the fourth Sunday in Lent. Try to discover its origins and why it was included in the Christian calendar in Lent.

3 Try to find out how Shrove Tuesday and Ash Wednesday got their names.

4 Discover how various Christians observe Lent, if at all. Interview Christians who belong to various churches and make a chart to show their replies.

5 '. . . a holy season of self-denial'. Discuss why some Christians might practise self-denial during Lent.

Holy Week

Read *Mark* 11:1–11, 14:12–26
Luke 19:28–40, 22:7–23
Matthew 21:1–11, 26:17–30

Palm Sunday is celebrated throughout the Christian Church at the beginning of Holy Week. Sometimes members of a congregation are presented with palm crosses, the sale of which may also bring employment to people in Third World countries.

Some groups of Christians join in processions along 'Palm Sunday Road' in Jerusalem, and all over the world processions may be staged, often including a donkey and ending in a church. Special hymns are also sung, for instance:

All glory, laud and honour
To Thee, Redeemer, King,
To whom the lips of children
Made sweet hosannas ring!

Thou art the King of Israel,
Thou David's royal Son,
Who in the Lord's name comest,
The King and blessed One.

The people of the Hebrews
With palms before Thee went
Our praise, and prayer, and anthems
Before Thee we present.

To Thee before Thy passion
They sang their hymns of praise;
To Thee now high exalted
Our melody we raise.

Theodulf of Orleans

Christians of the Orthodox Church collect palm crosses on Palm Sunday

The Thursday of Holy Week is known as Maundy Thursday and amongst the observances many churches have a special celebration of Holy Communion. Some Christians in one town depicted the events of Maundy Thursday and Good Friday in a rather unusual way:

CENOTAPH SETTING FOR 'LAST SUPPER'

THE cenotaph near Blackpool's North Pier became the Good Friday setting for the 'Last Supper' during a presentation of 'The Way of the Cross'. The open-air production, lasting about 1½ hours, included a 100-strong cast enacting scenes in a dozen town locations to portray the humiliation, dereliction and ultimate triumph of Christ's passion.

Blackpool's Metropole Hotel became Pilate's palace; steps outside came into use as the high priest's residence and nearby gardens became Gethsemane.

The ecumenical passion play began at the war memorial in Princess Parade, gradually winding around the streets to reach 'Calvary' at St John's parish church. It travelled up Church Street shopping precinct before passing the Grand Theatre and the Opera House on the way to the church.

It was at this point that the Crucifixion was depicted, followed by the burial and resurrection of Jesus.

ACTIVITIES

1 Ask any Christians you know to tell you about how their church celebrates Palm Sunday. If possible, get information from members of different Christian denominations.

2 Find any other hymns about Palm Sunday and discuss what the writers suggest about the significance of the events.

3 Some Christians like to meditate on the events of the first Holy Week on the appropriate days during the week leading up to Easter. Look up Mark 11:1–14:26, Luke 19:28–22:23 or Matthew 21:1–26:30. Write a brief diary of what may have happened from Sunday to Thursday of that week.

4 Start some coursework on the Christian celebration of either the whole of Holy Week or of one day of it (notice that Holy Week is continued in the next Topic). Show how the celebrations today reflect the teaching of the Gospels.

5 Try to find out the origin and meaning of the word 'Maundy'.

6 Find out what practices are associated with Maundy Thursday and also their connection with the Gospels.

Good Friday

Read *Mark* 14:53–15:47
Luke 22:66–23:56
Matthew 26:57–27:66

Holy Week continues with Good Friday, the day of the Crucifixion. For some, Good Friday is a working day like any other, for others it is a holiday. Some Christians might remember the Crucifixion in church in a special way, perhaps with a service lasting for three hours, others might take part in an open air procession or service. The observance of this day might involve long personal devotions or merely the eating of hot cross buns!

The following shows how the Christians of one town observe the events of Good Friday:

A prayer used before Holy Communion in the Church of England on Good Friday is:

> *And now we give you thanks because for our sins he [Jesus] was lifted high upon the cross, that he might draw the whole world to himself; and, by his suffering and death, became the source of eternal salvation for all who put their trust in him.*
>
> *The Alternative Service Book, 1980*

Worshippers during the open air Good Friday service

CHRISTIANS from Harborough churches joined together on Good Friday for the annual Act of Witness service.

Over 150 people from various denominations gathered at the town's Congregational Church before parading along High Street led by cross bearer Mr Richard Twiselton (St Nicholas, Little Bowden) for a service on The Square.

The Chairman of Market Harborough and District Council of Churches led the worship with help from representatives of the Baptist, Methodist, Congregational and Catholic Churches . . .

After the service a Hunger Lunch at the Baptist Church raised more than £100 for Christian Aid.

Look up the hymn about the Crucifixion which is featured in Topic 4. There is a well-known negro spiritual about the Crucifixion, which includes the following verses:

> *Were you there when they crucified my Lord?*
> *Were you there when they crucified my Lord?*
> *Oh! Sometimes it causes me to tremble, tremble, tremble;*
> *Were you there when they crucified my Lord?*
>
> *Were you there when they nailed him to the tree?*
> *Were you there when they nailed him to the tree?*
> *Oh! Sometimes it causes me to tremble, tremble, tremble;*
> *Were you there when they nailed him to the tree?*

ACTIVITIES

1 Discuss why you think this day is called Good Friday.

2 Carry out a survey amongst Christians to find out how they observe Good Friday.

3 Consider the prayer and hymn above. Discuss how Christians see themselves as involved in the death of Jesus.

4 Imagine newspaper headlines which might have appeared on the first Good Friday. Write an account of the trials and death of Jesus as a newspaper report.

5 Prepare a meditation for Good Friday. Include readings, hymns and prayers. Perhaps you could present the meditation at an assembly.

6

Forgive them, Father! They don't know what they are doing.	My God, my God, why did you abandon me?
I promise you that today you will be in Paradise with me.	Father! In your hands I place my spirit.

This is HOLY WEEK

HE IS RISEN

Four of the sayings of Jesus from the cross are shown above. Write an account of the Crucifixion in four paragraphs, each one including one of the above sayings.

7 Some Christians might put a poster such as this in a window of their home during Holy Week. 'He is Risen' would be displayed only on Easter Sunday. Discuss how effective you think this is as a statement of a Christian's faith.

Easter

Read *Mark* 16:1–20
Luke 24:1–49
Matthew 28:1–20

Although many people in Christian countries consider Christmas to be the major Christian festival, for most Christians the Easter period, including Good Friday and Easter Sunday, is the most important celebration.

Many of the customs and symbols connected with Easter are concerned with new life. Special services are held in churches, sometimes with all-night vigils, or occasionally out of doors at sunrise on Easter Sunday. Easter services in two different denominations are described on the next page.

Holy story to be re-enacted

AS THE sun rises on Easter Sunday, at 6.05am, it will be greeted by a re-enactment in Willow Park, Wigston, of the Resurrection.

The dramatisation, by Central Avenue Christian Church, will begin at 6am and it will tell the story of how some women, when visiting the tomb of their friend Jesus, found that same tomb open and empty, when they arrived early in the morning to embalm his body.

The story will be told in the language of the Bible and will include music, some of which has been written by members of the congregation.

After the drama, breakfast will be served at the church in Central Avenue between 6.30 and 7am.

My second Easter

I HAVE just celebrated Easter for the second time this year, by attending the Easter Night worship at a Russian Orthodox church in London.

Beginning at about 11 o'clock on the evening before their Easter Day, which this year fell weeks after the Easter Day in the calendar of the Western Churches, the service started with the Canon of Great Saturday being sung and read. The church was in darkness, except for the candles around the image of Christ in the winding sheet, which lay below the ornate royal doors. During the ninth ode a priest bore the winding sheet into the altar, behind the doors, and placed it on the throne where it would remain during Eastertide.

The congregation – most of whom were standing – crowded in the darkness, listening to the glorious singing of the unaccompanied choir as the Matins of Easter Night unfolded. An angelic choir could not have sounded sweeter.

At around midnight the royal doors opened and the priests came out, robed in white vestments and carrying a cross and the Gospels. Led by servers with candles, banners and icons, the procession left the church by a side door and wound its way to the West door which in its closed position symbolised the sealed tomb and the gates of paradise which will be opened to us by Christ's resurrection. The officiating priest censed the closed door and proclaimed the resurrection to all.

It was Easter Day. The Lord was risen. The church doors were flung open, the lights were put on, the members of the congregation lit the candles that each one held. The building was full of light; the world was full of light for Christ was risen. The ancient cry rang out in three languages – Russian, Greek, English – 'Christ is risen,' 'He is risen indeed.'

Easter is a joyful festival when special hymns are sung. A service may include the words spoken by a member of the clergy, 'Christ is risen!', to which the congregation replies, 'He is risen indeed. Alleluia!' Alleluia or Hallelujah, meaning 'Praise God' is often heard at Easter. An Easter garden, often made by children, may be displayed in a church.

Which parts of the Gospel accounts does this Easter garden illustrate?

ACTIVITIES

1 Interview Christians from various denominations to discover how they celebrate Easter.

2 Discuss how members of your group celebrate Easter (if you do!). What connection is there between your celebrations and the events of the first Easter Sunday?

3 Gather together examples of Easter cards. Display them, with notes about their significance.

4 Read again the accounts of the Resurrection from the three Gospels, then answer the following questions:

a) In which Gospel is the story of the walk to Emmaus recorded?

b) How many people are said to have seen the risen Jesus?

c) What differences are there in the stories and how would you account for them?

d) At the time the Gospels were written, what explanation was being given for the events of the first Easter day?

e) Why was the official explanation not logical?

f) What do you think finally convinced the disciples that Jesus was alive?

Jesus Christ is risen today,
   Hallelujah!
Our triumphant holy day,
   Hallelujah!
Who did once upon the Cross,
   Hallelujah!
Suffer to redeem our loss,
   Hallelujah!

Hymns of praises let us sing,
Unto Christ our heavenly King.
Who endured the Cross and grave,
Sinners to redeem and save:

But the pain which He endured,
Our salvation hath procured;
Now above the sky He's King,
Where the angels ever sing:

Sing we to our God above,
Praise eternal as His love,
Praise Him, all ye heavenly host,
Father, Son and Holy Ghost!

5 Read carefully these words from an anonymous fourteenth century hymn and then answer the following questions:

a) Which accounts from the Gospels are referred to in this hymn?

b) What is the meaning of 'Hallelujah'?

c) What titles are found here of Jesus? Which of them are found in the Gospels and what is their significance?

d) Why do you think that Easter is considered to be the main Christian festival?

6 Look back at the modern hymn in Topic 5. Find as many Easter hymns as you can. Find out when the hymns were written, and discuss how the language used has changed over the centuries.

The Problem of Evil

Read *Mark* 1:12–13, 3:20–30, 7:20–3
Luke 4:1–13, 11:14–26
Matthew 4:1–11, 15:18–20

In this section we shall consider some of the Christian concerns which emerge from a study of the Gospels. Many arise because the world is not as it was intended to be; there is injustice, inequality, cruelty, violence, selfishness and broken relationships. Christians believe that this was not God's intention for the world, but since human beings have a free will, they have chosen evil rather than good. The Gospels suggest that individuals are responsible, for evil comes from within a person (Mark 7:20–3, Matthew 15:18–20).

The Gospels further suggest that there is an evil power, the Devil, who tempts and can control people. Jesus was tempted by the Devil, or Satan, and he was accused by some opponents of being controlled by 'the chief of the demons'. Belief in Satan (a name meaning adversary, opponent or enemy) as a personal, spiritual power is to be found in the Old Testament, but only in the New Testament do the ideas of this personal, evil force develop. In the Gospels Satan is pictured as trying to destroy the work of Jesus, but the Crucifixion and Resurrection are shown as evidence of Jesus' victory over the powers of evil. The final victory of good over evil is illustrated here by Sir Jacob Epstein's sculpture at Coventry Cathedral.

St Michael defeating Lucifer

Some Christians do not believe in a personal Devil, preferring to think of the Biblical accounts as symbolising the struggle between good and evil. Over the centuries, it has been common to turn the Devil into a figure of fun, with horns and a forked tail.

In his well-known book *The Screwtape Letters*, C.S. Lewis has an interesting comment:

> *There are two equal and opposite errors into which our race can fall about the devils. One is to disbelieve in their existence. The other is to believe, and feel an excessive and unhealthy interest in them. They themselves are equally pleased by both errors and hail a materialist or a magician with the same delight.*
>
> C.S. Lewis, Preface to *The Screwtape Letters*

ACTIVITIES

1 Four names or titles for the Devil are to be found in the preceding section and in the readings. Make a note of them and find out their meanings.

2 Discuss C.S. Lewis' comment about devils.

3 Look up Mark 7:20–3 or Matthew 15:18–20 and answer the following questions:

   a) Name three immoral actions suggested in the passage.

   b) According to the passage, what causes such immoral actions?

   c) How do the Gospels personify evil?

   d) What do the Gospels suggest about how evil can be overcome?

   e) Do you think that belief in the Devil has any relevance in society today?

4 Look again at the newspaper headlines. Discuss the dangers of Satanism and the occult.

One of Jesus' temptations was to gain power by worshipping the Devil. There are people today who worship the Devil. This is called Satanism and together with various other aspects of the occult, features increasingly in newspapers. Christians often give warnings about the dangers of such practices:

Satanic rituals blighting lives of the young

Church occult warning

Devil seized controls, says killer driver

Satanist numbers rise as Christian Churches decline

Pupils quizzed about satanic sacrifice rites

Human Rights

Read *Luke* 1:46–56, 4:16–30
Matthew 7:12, 18:21–35

> *. . . disregard and contempt for human rights have resulted in barbarous acts which have outraged the conscience of mankind . . .*
>
> From the Preamble to the *Universal Declaration of Human Rights*

One of the results of evil in the world is the failure to treat fellow human beings with justice and compassion, and to deny them the rights which we insist on for ourselves.

The Gospels emphasise the importance of justice and equality. In the Magnificat, Mary speaks of God bringing down the mighty and lifting up the needy. This would be revolutionary at the time it was written. When Jesus preached in Nazareth, he quoted a prophecy from Isaiah, suggesting that he had been chosen '. . . to bring good news to the poor . . . to proclaim liberty to the captives . . . to set free the oppressed'. This emphasis on the rights of the underprivileged is to be found throughout Luke's Gospel and is still emphasised by the Christian Church as well as by humanitarian organisations.

> *All human beings are born free and equal in dignity and rights*
>
> *Article 1*
>
> *Everyone has the right to life, liberty and security of person*
>
> *Article 3*
>
> *Everyone has the right to a standard of living adequate for the health and well-being of himself and of his family, including food, clothing, housing and medical care and necessary social services*
>
> *Article 25*
>
> *Universal Declaration of Human Rights*

The Universal Declaration of Human Rights was approved in 1948, after the Second World War, by the United Nations.

An important saying of Jesus, known as the Golden Rule is 'Do for others what you want them to do for you'.

In the parable of the unforgiving servant, the suggestion is made that because of selfishness and an unwillingness to forgive other people, basic human rights are denied to them.

Prejudice of various kinds, which will be discussed in Topic 34, has added to the 'disregard and contempt for human rights' mentioned in the Universal Declaration. This man, waiting to register his vote in an African election, is declaring to the world that he is 'free and equal in dignity and rights'.

ACTIVITIES

1 If you can find a copy of the Universal Declaration of Human Rights, read it and make a note of any of the articles which remind you of the passages you have read from the Gospels.

2 Collect newspaper cuttings about the abuse of human rights. Produce a folder or posters to illustrate the problem in various parts of the world.

3 Make a list of the human rights which you consider are being ignored in various parts of the world. Investigate one of the examples in detail.

4 Find examples of Christian efforts to help the underprivileged. Form them into a collage for display, perhaps using quotations from the Gospels as headings.

5 Write a modern parable based on Matthew 18:21–35.

6 Use the parable as part of an assembly on the subject of human rights, together with a reading from the Gospels and suitable prayers and hymns.

7 The following extract is part of a prayer which forms an act of resolve on the subject of human rights:

> *It is our resolve to reaffirm our faith in fundamental human rights, in the dignity and worth of the human person, in the equal rights of men and women and of nations large and small.*
>
> **Lord, help us.**
>
> *. . . it is our resolve to practice tolerance and live together in peace with one another as good neighbours.*
>
> **Lord, help us.**
>
> Liverpool Cathedral

Suggest ways in which Christians, as individuals and with others, could carry out these resolves.

Morality in Society

Read *Mark* 1:1–8
  Luke 3:1–20, 6:20–49
  Matthew 3:1–12, 5–7

A group of teenagers, asked what they thought were the main problems in society today, included the following:

- Drug abuse
- Poverty
- Homelessness
- Crime
- Pollution
- Loneliness
- Broken homes
- Violence
- Prejudice
- Child abuse

In his preaching, John the Baptist was not afraid to criticise the behaviour of people of his day. He preached that people should repent and show their repentance by a change in moral attitudes. He reprimanded Herod Antipas who had married his brother's wife, and found himself in prison for doing so.

Jesus' criticisms were more general, aimed at

the hypocrisy of the time. His ethical teaching, for instance in the Sermon on the Mount, was very positive – do's rather than dont's. It was intended for his followers, rather than for society in general, it would seem. The Sermon on the Mount contains principles for Christian behaviour that can be applied in any period of history and in all societies.

When Christians speak out about injustice or what they consider to be low moral standards in society, they frequently make the headlines and are often criticised for being too 'political'.

Bishop speaks his mind

Bishop 'appalled' by lack of care for homeless

Bishop at funeral calls on IRA to lay down its arms

Clerics accuse Government of hurting the poor

Church attacks 'injustice of urban poverty'

Anti-union laws attacked by Bishops

ACTIVITIES

1 Look up the following words in a dictionary, and make a note of their meaning: morality, hypocrisy, ethical, principle.

2 Look again at the headlines above. Discuss whether you think that Christians should comment on moral attitudes in society today.

3 What might John the Baptist find to criticise in our society today? Make a list of topics and then compare it with what others have written.

4 Discuss the list of problems suggested at the beginning of this Topic. Do you agree with it? Are there any other problems that you would add?

5 Look through the Sermon on the Mount (Matthew's Gospel) or the Sermon on the Plain (Luke's Gospel) and make a list of ethical issues which you consider to be relevant in society today.

6 Divide into groups, each choosing a different issue which you have listed in 5 above. Find information to illustrate the issue from newspapers, magazines, etc. Produce a collage for display, with a suitable title.

7 Choose a moral issue about which a Christian might feel strongly. Write a letter to an MP, from a Christian standpoint, suggesting what you think Parliament should do about it.

Marriage

Read *Mark* 10:1–12, 12:18–27
    Luke 16:18
    Matthew 5:27–32, 19:1–12, 22:1–14, 25:1–13

A very serious moment in a marriage service. What vows are Sarah and David likely to be making?

- A commitment
- An addition: one plus one equals one
- A field of battle, not a bed of roses
- A sacrament
- A mantrap
- A mutual pledge to make a relationship work
- A triangle: a man, a woman and God
- A covenant of perseverance

You will have guessed that all the above comments concern marriage; they reflect very different attitudes to it. The following is an extract from the marriage service most frequently used in the Church of England. You will notice the connections with the readings from the Gospels.

> *The Scriptures teach us that marriage is a gift of God in creation and a means of his grace, a holy mystery in which man and woman become one flesh. It is God's purpose that, as husband and wife give themselves to each other in love throughout their lives, they shall be united in that love as Christ is united with his Church.*
>
> *Marriage is given, that husband and wife may comfort and help each other, living faithfully together in need and in plenty, in sorrow and in joy. It is given, that with delight and tenderness they may know each other in love, and, through the joy of their bodily union, may strengthen the union of their hearts and lives. It is given, that they may have children and be blessed in caring for them and bringing them up in accordance with God's will, to his praise and glory.*
>
> *In marriage, husband and wife belong to one another, and they begin a new life together in the community. It is a way of life that all should honour; and it must not be undertaken carelessly, lightly, or selfishly, but reverently, responsibly, and after serious thought.*
>
> *The Alternative Service Book,* 1980

Christian marriage is so important that it is considered to be a sacrament in some churches. Because of the importance of the vows made in a Christian marriage ceremony and in view of the teaching of Jesus, some churches will not marry divorcees. Similarly, some people today, if they do not have strong Christian beliefs, think that it is better to be married in a registry office.

44

ACTIVITIES

1 Arrange for any of the group who have attended a church wedding or a registry office ceremony to report on what happened. Compare the two ceremonies. Discuss your views about the suitability of each ceremony for a Christian couple.

2 Find a copy of a marriage service. List the vows that are made.

3 Discuss the comments made about marriage at the start of this Topic. Decide what they mean (you may need a dictionary) and whether you agree with them.

4 Read Mark 10:1–12 or Matthew 19:1–10 and answer the following questions:
   a) In which Old Testament book did Moses give permission for divorce?
   b) What is the suggestion in this passage about God's intention for men and women?
   c) What connection is given in the passage between divorce and adultery?
   d) In what sense is marriage considered to be a sacrament?
   e) What is your opinion about divorce?

5 There are proposals being made about the use of locations other than religious buildings and registry offices for weddings. There are also suggestions that a new church service is needed for those who have lived together before marriage. Discuss these two issues.

6 It has been suggested that, because he did not marry, Jesus was not in favour of marriage. Discuss this, in the light of the passages listed at the start of this Topic.

7 'Till death us do part'. Carry out a survey of opinions as to whether marriage should be life-long.

Children

Read   *Mark* 9:33–7, 10:13–16
   Luke 9:46–8, 18:15–17
   Matthew 18:1–5, 19:13–15

> . . . *whoever does not receive the Kingdom of God like a child will never enter it*

With the above words, Jesus showed his concern for children, and rebuked the disciples' apparent lack of concern. Jesus taught not only by words but also by example. He had frequently healed children. In the two passages given above, he used children to teach about the Kingdom of God.

Jesus also went on to say, 'If anyone should cause one of these little ones to lose his faith in me, it would be better for that person to have a large millstone tied round his neck and be thrown into the sea' (Mark 9:42, Luke 17:2, Matthew 18:6).

Despite two thousand years of Christian teaching and the existence of many international agencies which try to protect the rights of children, there are still many abuses of these rights in this country and throughout the world.

A United Nations declaration lists the rights of the child, and this is shown on the next page.

45

The right to affection,
  love, and understanding.
The right to adequate nutrition
  and medical care.
The right to free education.
The right to full opportunity
  for play and recreation.
The right to a name and nationality.
The right to special care, if handicapped.
The right to be among the first to
  receive relief in times of disaster.

The right to learn to be a useful member
  of society and to develop individual
  abilities.
The right to be brought up in a spirit of
  peace and universal brotherhood.
The right to enjoy these rights, regardless
  of race, colour, sex, religion, national,
  or social origin.

United Nations Declaration of the
Rights of the Child

Concern for children

ACTIVITIES

1 Discuss your opinions about why children's rights are disregarded.

2 Make a list of the ways in which children's rights are ignored.

3 Make a list of all the children's charities that you can think of.

4 Find out what you can about any one of the Christian children's charities. Discover how its aims reflect the teaching of Jesus.

5

> . . . the Kingdom of God belongs
> to such as these

Answer the following questions:

a) What event led to this saying of Jesus?

b) Give two examples of how Jesus showed concern for children.

c) What happened on one occasion when the disciples were arguing about greatness?

d) What do you think are the characteristics of children which led to Jesus' comment about the Kingdom of God?

6 Look again at the Declaration of the Rights of the Child. Do you agree with all the statements? Discuss any other rights you think should be added to it.

7 These are details from a Sunday School notice board on the island of Guernsey. Discuss your views about Christian education. Should Christian parents ensure that children are taught their faith?

EMMANUEL BAPTIST
Sunday School
Est. 1877
Sunday 9.45 a.m.

'Train up a child in the way he should go and when he is old he will not depart from it'

Proverbs 22:6

Family Relationships

TOPIC 31

Read *Luke* *2:41–52, 15:11–32*

Problems in family relationships have always existed. The account of Jesus in the Temple at the age of twelve demonstrates some of the problems of adolescence. In the well-known parable of the Lost Son, Jesus pictured some of the strained family relationships that existed in his own day. The process of growing up is never without its problems for both parents and young people, and if this is recognised and discussed the process can possibly be made a little easier.

The following is a prayer for understanding within families:

The National Family Trust, a Christian organisation which exists to encourage family life, suggested recently that members of most British families lead totally separate lives even though they are living in the same home. This is perhaps one of the many reasons for the breakdown of family life. The Trust believes that improved communication and conversation between family members within the home is essential if family life as we know it is to continue. It is important that young people and parents learn to talk to each other, in order to understand each other's problems.

Father of Jesus, give grace and understanding to all who live in families. May the spirit of peace settle between parent and child, brother and sister. May the young realise that the old may be wiser than they. May the old see how many of the young are trying to set up your kingdom on earth. And by their harmony, may they give glory to you, O Father, and to the Son, through the one Spirit, blest forever. Amen.

P.D. Reynolds (adapted)

A family communicating

ACTIVITIES

1 Make a list of causes of friction today between parents and adolescents. Compare your lists and discuss which of these are modern problems and which might have existed in the first century.

2 Read again Luke 2:41–52. Write a paragraph to illustrate what teaching (a) Christian parents and (b) Christian teenagers might find in this passage.

3 Discuss whether you agree with the suggestion of the National Family Trust that families need to talk together more if they are to stay together.

4 Make a list of other reasons for the breakdown of family life. Compare your suggestions and discuss them.

5 Read Luke 15:11–32 and answer the following questions:

a) What do you think is the main point of this parable?

b) Explain the actions of the younger son.

c) Write a character sketch of the elder son.

d) What teaching about family relationships do you find in this story?

6 Problem pages in magazines often deal with letters about problems concerning family relationships. Write such a letter. Then distribute each letter to another member of the group who should attempt a reply, using Christian principles to try to give practical advice.

Women in the Church

Read *Mark* 3:13–19
Luke 6:12–16, 8:1–3, 23:55–6
Matthew 10:1–4, 28:1–10

Jesus chose twelve apostles; they were all men. In the First century in Palestine, women were not encouraged to take part in trades or professions of any kind, and certainly not to be teachers or leaders in the communities in which they lived. It was therefore a very new idea for Paul to write the following in one of his letters, which in all probability was written before the Gospels:

> *. . . there is no difference between Jews and Gentiles, between slaves and free men, between men and women; you are all one in union with Christ Jesus.*
>
> Galatians 3:28

We are told by Luke that women followed and supported Jesus during his ministry. Women were the last of Jesus' followers at the Crucifixion, saw where he was buried and were the first to visit the empty tomb. According to Matthew, and the writer of the fourth Gospel, it was to women that Jesus first appeared after his resurrection. The struggle for women's rights has been a long one, even in western civilisations. Find out, for instance, when women were granted the right to vote in parliamentary elections in this country. It has taken even longer for equal rights to be recognised in the professions, and the debate still goes on about women in the Church. In all these matters, discussions have been made more difficult by those holding extreme feminist or male chauvinist views.

Many non-conformist churches have had women ministers for some time. Although it has been accepted in principle, the ordination of women as priests has not yet taken place in the Church of England. The Roman Catholic Church is very much opposed to such a development. The main arguments against the ordination of women are that Jesus chose male, not female apostles and that the priest who officiates at Holy Communion or Mass represents Jesus and therefore must be male.

It was not until the Twentieth century that some branches of the Church appointed women as stewards or deacons, lay readers or local preachers, ministers or priests. Only recently has an Anglican woman been appointed as a suffragan (assistant) bishop in the United States.

The Anglican Church in New Zealand has now appointed a woman as a diocesan bishop (in charge of an area). The photograph below shows the first women priests to be ordained in the United Kingdom.

The Rev Irene Templeton and the Rev Kathleen Young – the United Kingdom's first women priests, after their ordination into the Church of Ireland.

ACTIVITIES

1 Look up the meaning of: feminist, male chauvinist, suffragan, diocesan, ordination, officiate.

2 Make a list of reasons for and against the ordination of women as priests/ministers. Discuss your views.

3 Interview Christians from as many different denominations as possible to discover attitudes to the role of women in the various churches. First prepare questions, for example:

a) Do women act as church wardens/stewards/elders in your church?

b) Does your church have women ministers/priests?

Present your findings in the form of a chart.

4 Collect newspaper and magazine cuttings about the rôle of women in the church. Remember to include various denominations.

5 It might be possible to invite a woman minister or deacon to speak to your group on the subject of the rôle of women in the church. Perhaps you could also invite someone opposed to the ordination of women?

6 Discuss the contribution made in the Gospels to the issues above.

Concern for Those in Need

Read *Mark* 2:13–17
Luke 5:27–32, 7:36–50, 18:9–14, 19:1–10
Matthew 9:9–13, 25:31–46

There were many 'social outcasts' in New Testament times who, for various reasons, were shunned by their fellow Jews. They included tax collectors who worked for the Romans, petty criminals and women who were probably prostitutes. Their need was for forgiveness and friendship. Others in need included the poor, refugees, the sick and those in prison.

Jesus set an example for the treatment of such people and his teaching was very practical. Matthew records Jesus' teaching about the final judgement (25:31–46) which suggests ways in which Christians should put their faith into practice:

- Provide for the hungry and thirsty
- Give shelter to refugees
- Provide clothing for the needy
- Care for the sick
- Visit prisoners

Mother Teresa was once asked why she spent her life caring for the destitute and dying. Her reply was:

> *I see Christ in every person I touch because he has said, 'I was hungry, I was thirsty, I was naked, I was sick, I was suffering, I was homeless and you took me in . . .' It is as simple as that. Every time I give a piece of bread, I give it to Him.*
>
> Desmond Doig, *Mother Teresa – Her People and Her Work*

A prison chaplain in a maximum security prison describes his work:

> **'I was in prison and you visited me'**
> *In 1744 a man named Silas Todd began visiting prisoners in Newgate after hearing a sermon on these words. Many prisoners were changed by the influence of such visitors, but since you could be hanged for stealing a chicken in those days, they had little chance of putting any good back into society. When our prisons were reformed it was decided that each should have a chaplain to look after the prisoners' welfare. Nowadays many others are engaged in this: probation officers, teachers, psychologists. But the chaplains still look after spiritual welfare. They hold services, Bible classes and visit the prisoners in their cells or workshops. They are called on in times of trouble: when someone's relative dies, or his girlfriend jilts him, or he gets a 'Dear John' letter from his wife. Real friendships can be made, and people are still being changed by God's love. Such prisoners prove a real help to others when released.*

ACTIVITIES

1 Discuss what kinds of people might be considered 'outcasts' in our society.

2 Try to find examples from newspapers and magazines of people showing concern for such 'outcasts'. Mount and display the information you discover.

3 Discuss Mother Teresa's comment on Matthew 25:31–46.

4 Using the five points suggested by Jesus for putting Christian faith into practice, make a list of any organisations that you know about which put into practice the teaching given in Matthew 25:31–46.

5 Discuss where, in society today, there is most need for Christians to put their faith into action.

Prejudice

TOPIC 34

Read *Mark* 7:24–30

Luke 2:32, 3:6, 4:25–7, 7:1–10, 9:51–6, 10:13–14, 25–37, 13:29, 14:15–24, 17:11–19, 24:45–7

Matthew 8:5–13, 15:21–8, 28:18–20

You will have noticed that the vast majority of the above readings are from Luke's Gospel. It is thought that the author of this Gospel was a Gentile (non-Jew). He was certainly writing for someone with a Greek name, Theophilus (1:1)

and it seems that he wished to show that Jesus had come into the world for Gentiles as well as Jews.

There was a great deal of prejudice against Gentiles, for many Jews believed that they alone

were intended to have a special relationship with God. The Samaritans lived between Judaea and Galilee and were descendants of non-Jewish settlers. For most Jews, there would be no such person as a 'good Samaritan', which gives added point to the well-known parable told by Jesus.

The issue of prejudice is even more important in our multi-racial society than it was in the First century. Racial prejudice is not the only type of prejudice in our society. Prejudice is sometimes shown on the basis of sex, religion, politics or social class. Here is a modern prayer for harmony.

> *O Lord Jesus Christ, Prince of Peace, break down the barriers which separate men from each other and from God. Teach Christians to love each other across the walls of colour, class and creed: forgive us, too, for the excuses we make for our own prejudice. And lead us captive in your cause of peace on earth, good will to men. For your Name's sake. Amen.*
>
> Ian D. Bunting

ACTIVITIES

1 Discuss what is meant by prejudice. Look it up in a dictionary if necessary. Try to be honest about your own prejudices.

2 Look again at the above prayer. What excuses do people make for their prejudices? Make a list and then compare ideas.

3 Discuss the problems of racial prejudice and discrimination which you have experienced or heard about. What do you think should be a Christian's attitude?

4 Undertake a survey on prejudice of various kinds. List as many types of prejudice as you can think of and then make up relevant questions intended to reveal prejudices. Present the results as a class chart.

5 Read Luke 7:1–10 or Matthew 8:5–13 and then answer the following questions:
   a) What racial tension is shown in this passage?
   b) What efforts to overcome prejudice are illustrated here?
   c) Give two other examples of Jesus' actions which show that he did not have any racial prejudice.
   d) What would you consider to be the most common prejudices in our society today?
   e) What do the Gospels suggest about ways of overcoming prejudice?

Quakers called to 'help fight racism'

BRITAIN'S Quakers are being urged to help end racial prejudices in society – and to begin by overcoming prejudices within themselves.

A statement from the 200-strong Meeting for Sufferings – the denomination's governing body – calls on Quakers to strive to understand the problems of multi-racial communities, especially if they do not live in one themselves.

Describing the ways in which members of ethnic minorities suffer discrimination in today's Britain, the single-page document declares: "Being aware of injustice and doing little about it condones that injustice".

6 Read the above newspaper article. Discuss it. Do you agree that it is important to understand the problems of multi-racial communities if you do not live in one yourself?

7 Try to find out, from church magazines, newspapers or Christians you may know, about attempts that are being made to follow the example of Jesus in overcoming prejudice. Produce a collage of the information you find and display it.

The Problem of Suffering

Read *Mark* 10:32–4, 14:32–42, 15:21–37
Luke 13:1–5, 18:31–4, 22:39–46, 23:26–43
Matthew 5:45, 26:36–46, 27:32–44

The problem of human suffering has been discussed for centuries, and will certainly continue to be debated. If there is a God of love, why does he allow suffering in the world? One answer produced many centuries before Christ was that suffering is a punishment for sin. In an ancient poem, we are told that when Job, a God-fearing man, suffered very much, a friend suggested:

> *It is not because you fear God*
> *that he reprimands you and brings you*
>   *to trial.*
> *No, it's because you have sinned so*
>   *much;*
> *it's because of all the evil you do.*
>
> Job 22:4–5

> *. . . it is not I, your God, who has*
> *willed suffering, it is men.*
> *They have brought it into the world in*
> *bringing sin,*
> *Because sin is disorder, and disorder*
> *hurts.*
> *There is for every sin, somewhere in the*
> *world and in time, a corresponding*
> *suffering.*
> *And the more sins there are, the more*
> *suffering.*
> *But I came, and I took all your sufferings*
> *upon me, as I took all your sins,*
> *I took them and suffered them before*
> *you.*
>
> Michel Quoist, *Prayers of Life*

Job, and many people since, have decided that it is just not true to our experience that the wicked suffer and the righteous prosper. Jesus once spoke about victims of barbarity and accidents, stating that their sin was not greater than the sin of other people. He used the incidents to encourage those listening to him to repent (Luke 13:1–5).

Much of the suffering in the world is a result of human action and cannot be blamed on God. We all suffer, simply because we are human beings, with physical bodies and emotions which can be hurt. Christians believe that Jesus entered fully into our humanity, including its suffering.

The result of human action.

ACTIVITIES

1 List any recent disasters similar to the ones commented on by Jesus (Luke 13:1–5).

2 Look up John 9:1–3 and discuss Jesus' comment about suffering in that passage.

3 Make a list of different types of suffering and add a note about what you think is the cause of each type.

4 Collect newspaper cuttings about suffering and disasters. Make a collage and, if possible, list reasons why the suffering occurred.

5 Discuss the extract from the prayer of Michel Quoist. What connection does he suggest between sin and suffering?

6 Discuss the following comments about suffering:

> 6 The existence of suffering disproves the existence of God. 9

> 6 Suffering is a natural part of the human condition. 9

> 6 Every cloud has a silver lining. 9

> 6 Why should this happen to me? 9

> 6 Pain is basically good; it is a warning mechanism. 9

> 6 Much human suffering is a consequence of human free will. 9

7

> *If you will, take this cup of suffering away from me*

Answer the following questions:

a) On what occasion were these words spoken?

b) What is meant by 'this cup of suffering'?

c) What does this prayer teach Christians about their attitude to suffering?

d) What do you think is the teaching of the Gospels about suffering?

Healing

Read *Mark* 1:21–45 . . .
Luke 4:31–41 . . . 10:9
Matthew 8:1–17 . . . 25:31–6

The above are references to only a small number of the miracles of Jesus recorded in the Gospels. The fourth Gospel tells us that the disciples once asked Jesus whose sin had caused a man to be born blind (John 9:1–3). Jesus replied that his blindness had nothing to do with sin and went on to show his concern by healing the man. We are frequently told that Jesus was 'filled with pity' when he saw someone suffering. Compassion is only genuine when it leads to action, and Jesus used his power to heal on a number of occasions. For a discussion of the healing miracles, see *The Gospels Today*, Topic 12. The healing miracles of Jesus fall into three groups: general healing, exorcisms (casting out evil spirits) and raising the dead.

Luke records that when Jesus sent 72 disciples out on a mission, he gave them instructions to 'heal the sick'. The early Church practised healing by anointing and prayer:

> *Is there anyone who is ill? He should send for the church elders, who will pray for him and rub olive-oil on him in the name of the Lord. This prayer made in faith will heal the sick person; the Lord will restore him to health*
>
> James 5:14–15

Christians still pray for the sick, as this prayer shows:

> *Merciful Father, help all who suffer in pain of body or grief of heart, to find in you their help; and as Jesus suffered pain in his body and healed it in others, help them to find their peace in him, and by your mercy be renewed in strength of body and mind. Through Jesus Christ our Lord. Amen.*
>
> Dick Williams

Some Christians believe that they have the gift of healing. Various kinds of faith-healing or spiritual healing are practised, not only by the Christian Church. Conventional medicine was also pioneered by Christians, who established the first hospitals. Many missionary societies have had health care as one of their priorities.

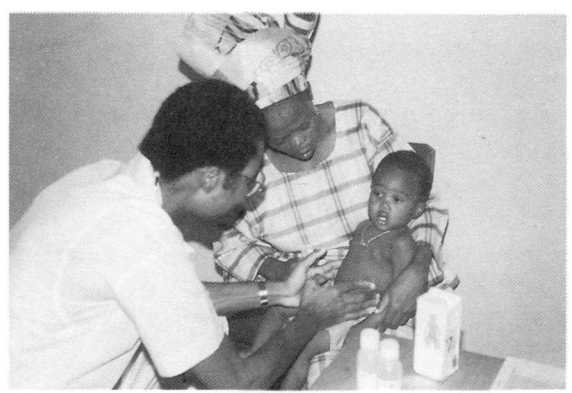

ACTIVITIES

1 Look through the Gospel(s) you are studying and make a list of the healing miracles in three columns, as follows:

Healing Miracles					
General	Ref.	Exorcisms	Ref.	Raising the Dead	Ref.
Simons' Mother-in-law	Mark 1:29-30	Man with an evil spirit	Mark 1:21-8	Jairus' daughter	Mark 5:35-43

2 Choose one type of illness or disability which you have listed above (e.g. blindness, deafness, paralysis). Find out about any charities which exist to help sufferers today. Perhaps you could present an assembly about what you have discovered?

3 Discuss the healing miracles of Jesus and any examples you know of modern 'miracles'.

4 Find out what you can about 'spiritual healing' today. Discuss the implications of what you discover.

5 Collect illustrations of Christians carrying out the command of Jesus, 'Heal the sick' (Luke 10:9). Make a poster to illustrate these words.

MIRACLE OP CURE

WOMAN'S MIRACLE FIGHT

Hunger

Read *Mark* 6:30–44, 8:1–13
Luke 3:10–14, 9:10–17, 16:19–31
Matthew 14:13–21, 15:32–9, 25:31–46

Photographs of starving children are often shown on television and in newspapers. The problem of world hunger should be decreasing as communications become easier and the need becomes known. However, the issue is complicated by such things as changes in climate, wars and other economic factors. It has been stated that each year the world's harvests are sufficient to feed one and a half times the world's population. Yet still there is hunger.

The words of Jesus 'You give them something to eat' (Mark 6:37) have encouraged people through the ages to provide for those in need. However, aid has not always been given in the most effective way, and the need is as great today as when the words were first spoken. This is how one Christian agency has used the miracle of the feeding of the five thousand to encourage Christians to help those in need:

God is still working miracles through people who are prepared to give up something.

ACTIVITIES

1 List the causes of food shortages. Make a note beside each as to whether and how you think the problem could be tackled.

2 Make a list of aid agencies which aim to provide food for people in need.

3 Choose one of the agencies listed and find information about it. If you write to the headquarters, be sure to include a donation to cover postage, etc. Perhaps you could organise a sponsored event to raise funds for the charity?

4 Discuss the use made of the account of the feeding of the five thousand in the above poster. How does it interpret the account?

5
> *Give a man a fish*
>   *and you feed him for a day.*
> *Teach a man to fish*
>   *and you feed him for life.*

Discuss what you think are the most practical ways of providing aid for people who are starving. Refer to the Chinese proverb above. What is the difference between short-term and long-term aid?

	Approximate % of the world's population	Approximate % of the world's wealth	Approximate % of the world's food supplies
Developed Countries	30	80	70
Third World	70	20	30

6 With reference to the above chart, answer the following questions:

a) Which are the developed countries?

b) What is meant by the Third World?

c) Write a paragraph on the unequal distribution of the world's food supplies.

d) What do you think should be the Christian response to the above statistics?

7

> *Whoever has food must share it*

Answer the following questions:

a) Who spoke these words?

b) To whom were they spoken?

c) Give an example of an occasion when Jesus gave practical help to people who were hungry.

d) Describe briefly one Christian response to the problem of hunger.

The Use of Force

Read *Mark* 11:15–17, 14:43–52

Luke 9:54–5, 15:1–32, 19:45–6, 22:35–8, 47–53, 23:32–43

Matthew 4:1–11, 5:21–6, 38–48, 18:23–35, 21:12–13, 26:47–56

‘If you can't get a job, you can always join the army.’

‘I am a pacifist: I believe that all killing is wrong.’

‘That makes me angry. Surely it is right to defend yourself if attacked by another country?’

‘I don't think so. There is too much violence in the world already, with terrorism, muggings and hooliganism. It only adds to the problem if you support violence officially in the form of war.’

‘But surely there would be much less violence if the death penalty were re-introduced . . .’

This snippet of a conversation reveals a number of ideas about the use of force. Throughout history there have been differences of opinion between those Christians who are pacifists and those who believe that it is right to take part in

a 'just' war. There is no direct teaching on this matter in the Gospels. When Jesus suggested that there should be no revenge, he was talking about personal relationships rather than inter-national affairs. However, if we all followed his advice to 'love your enemies' there would certainly be no war.

The problem of appropriate punishment for criminal offences is also one about which Christians disagree. There are those who believe that the reintroduction of the death penalty would act as a deterrent to violence; others feel that it would merely add to the violence in our society. These are situations where Christian principles of justice, love and forgiveness have to be applied.

ACTIVITIES

1 The Biblical references listed at the start of this Topic are about different aspects of violence. List them under the following headings:

- The use of force
- Non-resistance to violence
- Anger
- Love and forgiveness.

2 Discuss the issues raised in the con-versation at the start of this Topic.

3 Draw up two columns, listing all the points you can think of:

a) in favour of pacifism
b) against pacifism.

4 Discuss the complicated issue of world trade in armaments.

5

All who take the sword will die by the sword

Answer the following questions:

a) In which Gospel are these words found?
b) At what point in the life of Jesus were they first spoken?
c) What action led to this statement?
d) Do you think these words have any application in society today?
e) What different Christian attitudes have you heard expressed on the subject of war?

Wealth and Poverty

Read *Mark* 10:17–31

Luke 6:24, 12:13–34, 16:1–31, 18:18–30, 19:1–27

Matthew 6:19–34, 25:31–46

The gap between rich and poor is as great in the world today as when the Gospels were written. Luke's Gospel, in particular, emphasises the dangers of wealth and possessions, and res-ponsibilities towards the poor. A number of parables are recorded concerning wealth, as well as conversations which Jesus had with rich people. He demanded total commitment from his followers, and two of his sayings are, 'You cannot serve both God and money' (Luke 16:13, Matthew 6:24), and 'Sell all your belongings and give the money to the poor' (Luke 12:33).

We live nowadays in a society where wealth and material possessions have become all-important to many people, but this concern with affluence does not necessarily lead to personal happiness.

Christian Aid is one of many charities which encourage people to share their wealth with the poor both in this country and abroad.

A Hong Kong refugee camp

ACTIVITIES

1 Discuss people's attitudes to possess-ions. Do you see any dangers in living in an affluent, materialistic society?

2 With reference to the readings from the Gospels, answer the following questions:

a) Name two parables in which there is teaching about the dangers of wealth.

b) Name a parable in which there is teaching about the use of wealth.

c) What did Jesus say would happen to those who '. . . pile up riches for themselves but are not rich in God's sight'?

d) Who was told '. . . Sell all you have and give the money to the poor'?

e) What, according to the Sermon on the Mount, is the antidote to worry-ing about material things?

f) What do you think Jesus meant by '. . . make friends for yourselves with worldly wealth'?

3 Answer each part of this essay:

a) Describe briefly two occasions when rich people spoke with Jesus.

b) What was Jesus' teaching about wealth?

c) What application do you think this teaching has for Christians today?

4
> *You will always have poor people with you, and any time you want to, you can help them.*
> Mark 14:7

Which groups of people would you consider to be poor in society today? Carry out a group survey to find out what is being done to help them in your community. If possible, arrange interviews with representatives from various local churches, charities, the social services and so on. Display your results on a chart.

5 Discuss the sayings of Jesus concern-ing wealth which you have found in this Topic.

Attitudes and Motives

Read *Mark* 12:28–34
      Luke 10:25–36
      Matthew 5:1–12, 21–30, 43–8, 6:1–4, 7:24–9, 22:32–40, 25:31–46, 28:18–20

A Christian is someone who:

- believes in Jesus Christ
- goes to church
- follows the teaching of Jesus
- can say the Apostles' Creed
- has been taken over by the Spirit of Jesus
- follows the rules of the church
- trusts Jesus as Saviour and Lord
- loves God and other people

A number of the above definitions of a Christian may well be true; think about them in view of what you have read in the above passages from the Gospels.

The Sermon on the Mount suggests that a person's thoughts and motives are as important as actions (Matthew 5:21–48). The Beatitudes (Matthew 5:3–12) imply that the relationship a person has with God produces a Christian character. Such a relationship motivates a person to obey the instructions of Jesus (Matthew 7:24–30), including his last command to his disciples:

> *Go, then, to all peoples everywhere and make them my disciples: baptise them in the name of the Father, the Son and the Holy Spirit, and teach them to obey everything I have commanded you.*
>
> Matthew 28:19–20

There was some discussion at the time of Jesus as to whether the offering of sacrifices or the offering of personal devotion was the most important aspect of the Jewish faith. Jesus' teaching was that love for God and for others should be the motivation for all our actions.

The Salvation Army – love in action.

ACTIVITIES

1 Discuss the definitions of a Christian given at the start of this Topic.

2 Look up the *Shema* (Deuteronomy 6:4–5). This is an important Jewish statement which was quoted by Jesus. Discuss it.

3 Look up Matthew 5:21–48. Write a paragraph about Jesus' teaching on attitudes and actions.

4 Talk informally to any Christians you know to find out how their faith affects their lives.

5 Find and read a biography of a Christian. Work out what was the motivation for the person's life.

6 Write an essay about the connection between:
   a) Christian belief
   b) Christian observances, such as church attendance
   c) personal devotion
   d) Christian action.

7 Discuss how these two verses of a modern hymn show the connection between the four points above. Find other Christian hymns or prayers which show the connection between faith and life.

The Servant King

From heav'n you came, helpless babe,
Enter'd our world, Your glory veil'd;
Not to be served but to serve,
And give Your life that we might live.

   This is our God, the Servant King,
   He calls us now to follow Him,
   To bring our lives as a daily offering
   Of worship to the Servant King.

So let us learn how to serve,
And in our lives enthrone Him;
Each other's needs to prefer,
For it is Christ we're serving.

Graham Kendrick

APPENDICES

Cross-references to *The Gospels Today*   **A**

This appendix is intended as a ready means of cross-reference between the subjects covered in this book and those covered in the companion volume *The Gospels Today: An Approach to the Synoptic Gospels for GCSE* (also by Eileen Bromley and published by Stanley Thornes).

Christian Issues in the Gospels		*The Gospels Today*		*Christian Issues in the Gospels*		*The Gospels Today*	
Topics	1	Topics	15, 21	Topics	21	Topics	8
	2		6, 8		22		9
	3		9, 13, 16		23		21, 22
	4		24		24		23, 24
	5		25		25		25
	6		19, 25		26		9, 14
	7		6, 8, 9, 14, 17		27		6, 11, 14, 15
	8		11, 16, 22, 25		28		9, 15
	9		6, 7, 9, 20		29		11, 19
	10		12, 21		30		18, 19
	11		9, 12, 18		31		7, 20
	12		9		32		10, 25
	13		22		33		10, 11, 14, 17, 19
	14		14		34		12, 13, 20
	15		17, 18		35		18, 23, 24
	16		18		36		12, 13
	17		15, 19		37		11, 13, 20
	18		20, 21		38		20, 21, 22, 23
	19		6		39		11, 15, 17, 20, 21
	20		7		40		11, 15, 20, 21, 25

Biblical Index

MARK'S GOSPEL

Reference	Topics
1:1–11	3, 7, 9, 12, 28
1:12–13	22, 26
1:14–20	15
1:21–45	17, 36
2:1–17	9, 11, 33
2:23–3:6	14
3:13–19	32
3:20–30	7, 26
4:35–41	3
5:25–43	10, 11
6:5–6	11
6:14–16	3
6:30–46	17, 37
7:20–3	26
7:24–30	34
8:1–13	17, 37
8:27–9:13	3, 15
9:14–29	11
9:30–41	16, 30
10:1–12	29
10:13–16	30
10:17–31	15, 39
10:32–45	16, 35
10:46–52	11
11:1–11	23
11:15–17	38
11:20–5	11, 17
12:18–27	10, 29
12:28–34	40
12:41–4	18
13:1–27	6, 19
14:12–26	4, 13, 23
14:32–42	17, 35
14:43–52	38
14:53–15:47	6, 24
15:21–41	4, 17, 35
16:1–20	6, 25

LUKE'S GOSPEL

Reference	Topics
1:5–80	2, 3, 7, 9, 19, 27
2:1–20	20
2:29–32	9, 34
3:1–23	3, 7, 9, 12, 28, 34, 37
4:1–14	7, 22, 26
4:16–30	7, 14, 27, 34
4:31–41	36
5:1–11	15
5:27–32	11, 15, 33
6:1–11	14
6:12–16	17, 32
6:20–49	28, 39
7:1–10	11, 34
7:18–34	3
7:36–50	9, 11, 33
8:1–3	32
8:22–5	3
8:43–56	10, 11
9:7–36	3, 37
9:43–56	16, 30, 34, 38
9:57–62	15
10:9	36
10:13–14	34
10:21–2	7, 17
10:25–37	34, 40
11:1–13	9, 17
11:14–26	26
12:13–38	18, 39
12:41–8	18
13:1–5	35
13:29	34
14:15–24	34
14:25–35	15
15:1–32	9, 38
16:1–13	18, 39
16:18	29
16:19–31	37
17:3–4	9
17:5–6	11
17:11–19	11, 34
18:1–14	17, 33
18:15–17	30
18:18–30	39
18:31–4	16, 35
18:35–43	11
19:1–27	9, 18, 29, 33, 39
19:28–40	23
19:45–6	38
20:27–40	10
21:1–4	18
21:25–8	6
22:7–23	4, 13, 23
22:31–46	17, 35, 38
22:47–53	38
22:66–71	6, 24
23:1–56	4, 17, 24, 32, 35, 38
24:1–49	7, 17, 25, 34
24:50–3	6

MATTHEW'S GOSPEL

Reference	Topics
1:18–25	1, 3, 7, 20
2:1–12	21
2:41–52	31
3:1–12	28
3:13–17	3, 7, 12, 21
4:1–11	7, 22, 26, 38
4:18–22	15
5–7	28, 40
5:21–6	17, 38
5:27–32	29
5:38–48	38
6:5–15	9, 17
6:19–34	39
7:7–11	17
7:12	27
7:13–14	10
8:1–17	11, 34, 36
8:23–7	3
9:1–2	11
9:9–13	15, 33
9:18–26	10, 11
10:1–4	32
11:2–6	3
14:13–21	37
15:18–20	26
15:21–8	11, 34
15:32–9	37
16:13–28	3
17:1–13	3
17:22–3	16
18:1–5	30
18:15–20	17
18:21–35	9, 27, 38
19:13–15	30
20:17–19	16
21:1–11	23
21:12–13	38
22:1–14	29
22:23–40	10, 40
24:29–31	6
24:45–51	18
25:1–13	29
25:14–30	18
25:31–46	33, 36, 37, 39, 40
26:17–30	4, 13, 23
26:36–46	17, 35
26:47–56	38
26:57–75	6, 24
27:1–66	4, 24, 35
28:1–15	25, 32
28:16–20	7, 12, 25, 34, 40

Index